Max Davidson is a novelist, critic and journalist, who writes extensively for the *Daily Telegraph* and other national newspapers. His novels include *The Wolf, Beef Wellington Blue, Suddenly in Rome* and *The Greek Interpreter*. At different times in his life, he has been a House of Commons Clerk, a restaurant critic, a TV reviewer and a travel writer. He is also a lifelong armchair sports fan, with the passion and argumentativeness of the breed.

Alex,
Congratulations!
Continue to work hard and do your best and you will be a winner in all things!
Mr Harbeu

It's Not the Winning that Counts

The most inspiring moments of sporting chivalry

MAX DAVIDSON

ABACUS

First published in Great Britain in 2009 by Little, Brown
This paperback edition published in 2010 by Abacus

A CIP catalogue record for this book
is available from the British Library.

ISBN 978-0-349-12207-6

Typeset in Garamond by M Rules
Printed and bound in Great Britain by
Clays Ltd, St Ives plc

Papers used by Abacus are natural, renewable and
recyclable products sourced from well-managed forests and certified
in accordance with the rules of the Forest Stewardship Council.

Mixed Sources
Product group from well-managed
forests and other controlled sources
www.fsc.org Cert no. SGS-COC-004081
© 1996 Forest Stewardship Council

FSC

Abacus
An imprint of
Little, Brown Book Group
100 Victoria Embankment
London EC4Y 0DY

An Hachette UK Company
www.hachette.co.uk

www.littlebrown.co.uk

For Clara, finally

Contents

Acknowledgements

One of the most enjoyable things about writing this book has been picking the brains of fellow sports-lovers. You will not find acts of sportsmanship in the record books: they are lodged in the memory of fans, and I am grateful for the elephantine powers of recall of, among others, Glen Dwyer, Richard Evans, Sally Laurence Smyth, Matt Zuckerman, Jim White, Douglas Millar, Peter Flynn, John Riley, Gillian Johnson, Crispin Poyser, David Levine, Philip Ruttley, Andrew Robson, David Crouch, Clive Batty, Colin Lee, Philip de Ste Croix, that nice barman in the gastropub in Bristol, and my tennis-forum buddies 'Burrow', 'Zolka' and 'Mrs Fedex'. Without their contributions and suggestions, several of the stories in the book would have slipped through my net.

I would particularly like to thank the sportsmen featured in the book who took the time to share their memories with me: Steve Kember, Pete Goss, Alex Stepney, John Francome, Robin Dixon and Sir Stirling Moss. For a sports groupie like me, every second in their company was a delight.

Of the books I have read in the course of my researches and, in many cases, quoted, the following were invaluable and are warmly recommended: *Play up Corinth* by Rob Cavallini; *Sir Gary* by Trevor Bailey; *The Story of the Davis Cup* by Alan Trengove; *The Perfect Mile* by Neal Bascomb; *Close to the Wind* by Pete Goss; *The First Forty Years* by Tony Jacklin; *Ted Williams* by Leigh Montville; *Walking to Victory* by Adam Gilchrist; *Sport and the British* by Richard Holt; *White King and Red Queen* by Daniel Johnson; *Born Lucky* by John Francome; *The Larwood Story* by Harold Larwood; *Life Swings* by Nick Faldo; *Their Day in the Sun* by Doris H. Pieroth; *Herbert Sutcliffe* by Alan Hill; *William Marshal: Knighthood, War and Chivalry* by David Crouch; and *The Greatest* by Muhammad Ali.

Although I have been sports-mad since I was a schoolboy, and a published author for more than twenty-five years, I have never written professionally about sport, so it was brave of Richard Beswick at Little, Brown to take on such an unknown literary quantity. He has been an enthusiastic but exacting editor, and I am much indebted to the rest of the team at Little, Brown – notably Iain Hunt, Rowan Cope and Linda Silverman – who have helped bring the project to fruition.

Like all writers, I have gone through periods of self-doubt. I *thought* I had hit on a cracking idea for a sports book. But suppose readers found my love of chivalry impossibly old-fashioned and sentimental? Luckily, I have been sustained throughout by the support and encouragement of loved ones. My elder daughter, Anna, a medical student, could not tell a leg-break from a sprained ankle, but has been inspirational in her blood-and-guts determination. My younger daughter, Clara, is good sportsmanship personified. Last but not least, my long-suffering Australian partner Julia has borne my many eccentricities with fortitude and good humour. How many of her countrywomen have to put up with blood-curdling cries of 'How*zat*!' every time Ricky Ponting is hit on the pads?

Introduction

Iconic images matter. Football fans always feel a glow of pleasure when they look at the photograph of Pele and Bobby Moore exchanging shirts after the Brazil-England match at the 1970 World Cup. Here, in perfect miniature, is the beautiful game that Pele talked about. The photograph does not give pleasure because the two players featured in it happen to be famous but because of the bond of good fellowship between them. Which side won the match? If you did not know, you would never guess from the body language. There is not the faintest whiff of sour grapes, that most toxic element in the footballing brew.

In an alcove in my kitchen, opposite my favourite armchair, is a framed photograph of another iconic sporting moment: Freddie Flintoff consoling Brett Lee after the 2005 Edgbaston Test. The photograph is reproduced above. I must have looked at the picture a thousand times, the way a monk might look at the crucifix on the wall of his cell. It has become a touchstone, a distillation of everything I hold dear.

At the going down of the sun and in the morning, I steal a glance at Flintoff's kind, generous face, and I feel a little bit better about the world. And I am not ashamed of that. In a faithless age, we all have to find our own gods.

What deliriously sweet memories the photograph stirs! The seventh of August 2005, the day it was taken, was my fiftieth birthday. I spent the morning visiting my father in a geriatric ward in Tooting. When I arrived at the hospital, with *Test Match Special* on the car radio, it looked as if England, for the umpteenth time against Australia, were about to snatch defeat from the jaws of victory. When I left an hour later and turned on the radio, heart pounding, I heard the good news: England had won by just two runs, the narrowest margin in Ashes history. No birthday present ever felt sweeter. It seemed providential.

All day long the pleasure of a famous victory burned within me, like a fire that could not be quenched. It was not until the next morning that the significance of the Flintoff–Lee moment – which had been missed by the TV cameras, but captured by a stills photographer, Tom Shaw – sunk in. Joy upon joy. An English sporting champion giving a lesson in English sportsmanship! Did the Aussies behave as well as this when they were thrashing us? In victory, magnanimity . . . It was as if Churchill's great phrase had been made flesh in the burly figure of Flintoff.

If it had been another England player consoling Lee, the photograph would have had less significance. It was the fact that it was Freddie – Mr Infredible, as the *Daily Mirror* hailed him – the man whose heroics with bat and ball had swung the match, that made millions of us swell with patriotic pride. How often had we been taunted that we would never win anything because we were too English, too nice, too soft. Here, suddenly, was victory, an English victory, with the softest of soft centres, as if in dignified rebuke to our critics.

Suddenly I was a schoolboy again, aflame with hero-worship. You can laugh at a middle-aged man feeling those emotions so keenly, but I was hardly the only person to be smitten by the big Lancastrian. After a heart-stopping victory, topped off by this daintiest of grace notes, he was a hero to millions.

And what a hero, straight from a comic book. On the Saturday of the Test, Flintoff put his shoulder out and was in so much pain he could hardly hold his bat. Did he retire hurt? Did he hell. He just gritted his teeth, had 'a jab in me bum' in the lunch interval, then came out and biffed six after six. The Freddie myth grew and grew, as stories about his exploits proliferated. In the dressing room after play, as the players shared a beer, there was no bottle-opener to be found. Was Freddie thwarted? Not on your life. He just opened the bottles with his teeth. Popeye, eat your heart out.

But no Popeye cartoon can hold a candle to the Flintoff–Lee photograph. You could know nothing of cricket, nothing of what happened at Edgbaston, and still be struck by this image: one human being reaching out, with compassion and tenderness, to comfort another. A simple geometric detail holds the key to its power. The face of the comforter, Flintoff, is an inch or two lower than the face of the man he is comforting, Lee. The Australian is right down on his haunches, and Flintoff is an enormous man, six foot five, but still he has stooped so low that he is looking up into the eyes of Lee. This is not the kind of pity that patronises: someone feeling sorry for someone else, the way the rich man might feel sorry for the beggar. It is the real thing, rooted in humility.

When I was a cricket-obsessed schoolboy, devouring every book about the game I could lay my hands on, one of the Victorian cricketers who fascinated me was Alfred Mynn, of Kent and England, who pre-dated W. G. Grace. He was a tall, commanding figure, a gentle giant, and is commemorated in a charming obituary poem, which ends:

> . . . And as the changing seasons pass,
> As our Champion lies a-sleeping underneath the
>   Kentish grass,
> Proudly, sadly, we will name him – to forget him
>   were a sin –
> Lightly lie the turf upon thee, kind and manly Alfred
>   Mynn.

Kind and manly. Not kind *or* manly, a nice guy or a macho guy, a Tom Hanks or a Bruce Willis. Kind *and* manly. Is that not the elusive combination which all men strive for? And which Flintoff, unforgettably, displayed at Edgbaston?

Look closer at the photograph, and other details start to register. That big butch guy has a stud in his ear. Ah-ha! So our he-man hero has a lurking feminine side. He knows that it's all right to show your feelings. And the other man, the one he is comforting . . . Why is his forearm bruised and bloodied? Because he has just been battered by 90 mph bouncers by the man now consoling him. The two men may be locked in chivalrous embrace, but they have spent the last four days trying to knock each other's heads off.

Even the background to the main picture – spectral figures on their feet, clapping and cheering – adds to the drama of the composition. It is the paying spectators who make professional sport what it is: a great public stage on which the actors can cover themselves in glory or ignominy.

Commentators were quick to seize on another point. Flintoff had commiserated with Lee first, before celebrating with his team-mates. The other England players, naturally enough, mobbed the wicket-keeper, Geraint Jones, who had snaffled the vital catch, and the bowler, Steve Harmison. It was Flintoff who spotted Lee slumped in despair and went to console him. The choreography felt not just apt, but out of synch with the times. How often, when Tiger Woods wins a golf tournament, does he do a war dance with his caddie before shaking hands with his opponent, almost as an afterthought? Footballers the same. Shrill triumphalism is the *leitmotiv* of the age. Flintoff, quite spontaneously, found a better way. It felt like a throwback to the great days of sport, when playing the game was more important than winning.

In a summer etched in the memory, that same generosity of spirit suffused the whole Ashes series – contested, noted the editor of *Wisden*, with 'the perfect mix of chivalry and venom'. The high drama of England regaining the Ashes was accompanied by feelings of awe, astonishment and gratitude. Gratitude that sport in the twenty-first century, so often mired in cheating and controversy, could still make the headlines for the right reasons. Gratitude that a silly old game of bat-and-ball could still offer parables of good behaviour that brought a lump to the throat.

We had thought we were living in a debased age, condemned to a life of regret for the days when good manners graced the sports field, when nobody swore at anyone and none of the players wore sponsors' logos. Flintoff, in an instant, hit that lazy nostalgia for six. Sportsmanship was not dead. It had been there all along, below the surface, waiting to flower.

It's Not the Winning that Counts is a celebration of chivalry in sport, from Ancient Greece to the present day. It is a theme which, I hope, will strike a chord with other sports lovers, who are an old-fashioned, sentimental, moral tribe. They want their teams to win, but they want them to win in the right, sporting way: if they cheat in the process, or are graceless in victory, it leaves a residue of dissatisfaction. Nothing sours a victory sing-song more than the knowledge that victory was undeserved or tarnished by bad manners. The worse some professional sportsmen behave, the more the watching millions cling to the simple, child-like ideals that drew them to sport in the first place.

A sporting villain can add spice to the drama, like a baddie in a movie. At the Beijing Olympics, the Cuban Tai Kwon Do competitor who kicked the referee in the head provided one of the abiding images of the games – five-star entertainment, gruesomely hilarious. But it is when the villains run the whole show – when drug cheating becomes endemic, or when entire football teams are composed of divers and shirt-pullers – that the fun goes out of sport. That is when the good guys, the ones who abhor cheating, need to show their mettle.

This is not a tale of winning and losing; of plucky underdogs and gallant comebacks; of hat-tricks, holes-in-one and record-breaking times. There will be very few statistics in the book. It is a tale of magnanimity: sportsmen and women, on a great public stage, acting with an unforced, unrehearsed decency that seemed to embody the essence of sport.

As professional athletes, they had spent years honing their skills so that, in the pressure cooker of a big match, they could do what they were paid to do: serve an ace; slot home a penalty; cling on to a slip catch. But they did not learn sportsmanship on the training pitch. It came to them – or did not come to them – as naturally as breathing. They were ambushed by situations for which they were not prepared – an opponent getting injured, say – and had to respond to them as they saw fit. They had no time to consult the rule book and, even if they had, the rule book would have been no help. They had to listen to their hearts.

In most cases their actions were unpremeditated, the work of seconds. But the impact of such gestures, once they have entered sporting folklore, can be measured in years, even decades. Such little moments of chivalry remind us why sport matters. They fortify us against the voice of cynicism. 'They're all cheats.' 'They're only in it for the money.' They raise our sights above the day-to-day banalities of sport: who loses and who wins, who is in, who is out.

Some of the moments of sportsmanship featured in the book are already iconic, like the putt which Jack Nicklaus conceded to Tony Jacklin at the end of the 1969 Ryder Cup; others have dimmed with time. Who now remembers Bobby Pearce, Jess Sweetser, Cleveland Stroud, Mohammed Ali Rashwan, Judy Guinness? But I have tried to capture the human essence of each moment, so that it can be savoured in tranquillity.

My researches concentrated initially on football, the world game, and cricket, the English national game. But other sports quickly came into play – golf, tennis, boxing, athletics, rugby, even fringe sports like chess and mountaineering. Bobby Jones, Gary Sobers, David Beckham, Nick Faldo, Shane Warne . . . Some of the biggest names in sport stride across these pages. But you do not have to be a great sportsman to be a great sport. From Egyptian judokas to American softball players, Norwegian skiing coaches to

Australian scullers, bit-part players have also captured the public imagination with their gallantry and good humour.

Whenever two or more sportsmen are gathered together, the possibility of sportsmanship is present in their midst. Even non-participants can embody sporting chivalry. I have found space in the book – and I hope justifiably – for a Scottish bookmaker, a member of the Royal Family, a seventy-two-year-old Welsh mother-in-law, even twenty thousand fair-dinkum Sydney cricket fans.

When I began researching the book I expected to find that the most conspicuous examples of sportsmanship belonged to the amateur era, and had been inspired by the Corinthian spirit beloved of sporting romantics. The decline of good behaviour in an age of millionaire sportsmen is a commonplace of media pundits: they like to hark back to Jack Hobbs and Fred Perry and Stanley Matthews, the no-nonsense heroes of the cigarette cards, with their modest smiles and short-back-and-sides haircuts. It was gratifying to uncover a more complicated narrative. Freddie Flintoff is not the only modern sportsman to wear a halo. Here are Paolo di Canio, Pete Goss, Adam Gilchrist, Jan Ullrich, and many more. In fact, of the fifty-odd moments of outstanding sportsmanship I have chosen to highlight, nearly half took place in the last twenty years, within recent memory.

Urban myths die hard. To my surprise and delight, the more I examined the evidence, the more sceptical I became of the conventional wisdom – that sportsmanship has somehow become outmoded, like men holding doors open for women. There is a lot of mean-spiritedness in modern sport. It would be foolish to pretend otherwise. But then sport has *always* brought out the worst in people as well as the best. Some of the founding fathers of modern sport – W. G. Grace, to name but one – were anything but model sportsmen. At the 1904 Olympics in St Louis, one of the marathon runners hitched a lift on a truck. Football in its infancy was brutal. Throughout the long history of sport, there have been people who played the game in the right spirit and people who bent the rules to gain an advantage. Human nature changes less than the headline-writers allow.

In a strident age, it is easy to lose sight of qualities such as honesty, kindness, generosity, compassion, courtesy – the virtues which this book is celebrating and which are found in all human societies at all times. It would be a shame if we talked ourselves into a state of inconsolable pessimism about the direction sport is heading.

Professionalism may have brought some nasty habits in its wake, from drug-taking to the disrespect of match officials, but it has not stilled, can never still, the drumbeat of all sport, amateur and professional alike – fierce competition ending in a smile, a handshake and a post-match beer.

To Freddie Flintoff, and to others who have enshrined that spirit, this book is dedicated.

Come Back, Steve Kember

Welcome to the madhouse.

It is quarter past three on Saturday 20 September 2008. Watford are playing Reading in the Coca-Cola Championship, the second tier of English football. Not a crunch match, but a local, or reasonably local, derby, played in brilliant sunshine in front of an enthusiastic crowd, high with start-of-the-season optimism. There is no hint of the impending chaos, an incident of such surreal lunacy that, even though this is not a high-profile match, it will be splattered across the back pages.

A Reading shot is deflected wide of goal by a Watford defender. Another Watford player hooks the ball back into play, trying to prevent a corner, but is too late – the ball has already crossed the line, a couple of yards wide of the goal post. The assistant referee flags. The referee whistles. Everyone thinks a corner has been given. When the referee, after consulting his assistant, awards a goal, mayhem breaks out. What planet are the officials living on? Are they both blind?

If this were a kick around in the park everyone would collapse laughing. Jokes about referees and opticians would ring across the pitch. The fact that the referee is aged just twenty-five – he is a high-flier, the Pitt the Younger of his profession – would be the source of good-natured banter. Justice would be done, without fuss, and play would carry on. But when did a professional footballer – and this is the ingredient in the cocktail that leaves a bitter aftertaste – last see the funny side of things? They are hardwired to be attritional, uncompromising, mirthless.

The Reading players, hardly able to believe their luck, skulk back to the halfway line. The Watford players, terrified of being booked for dissent, follow sullenly after. Play resumes and the match finishes 2-2 – a score draw on the pools coupons, but we all know what a joke that is. In a just world, there would be an asterisk the size of a football against the first Reading goal.

Who to blame? Well, one could name and shame the officials, but that would be to join in the madness. What shame is there in their actions? They have made a mistake, a schoolboy howler, but it is an honest mistake. They are fools, not knaves – although you would never know that from the abuse that gets directed at them, both on the pitch and in the papers the next day, where pundits line up to pillory them for their ineptness. There are dark, rebellious mutterings. How can the FA demand respect for its officials when its officials are so incompetent? When are the referee and his assistant going to apologise? Who appointed them? What disciplinary sanctions do they face?

As the recriminations fly, people miss the simple, obvious truth. The real knaves – not because they have deliberately cheated, but because they have cynically profited from the blunder by the officials – are the Reading players.

'What can you do?' shrugs Reading captain Stephen Hunt after the match. 'You can't say, no, ref, that wasn't in.' From his manager, Steve Coppell, come feeble platitudes about playing to the whistle. The washing of hands is accompanied by protestations of impotence. *Don't blame us, we had no choice.*

In reality, of course, they did have a choice. They could simply have done the sporting thing and told the referee that it was not a goal.

If the officials were tricked by an optical illusion, the players fell victim to a different kind of illusion: that they were not responsible for the mistake, so they had no responsibility for rectifying it.

Even the Watford manager, Adrian Boothroyd, whose team have been unfairly penalised, follows the same warped logic. After the match, having directed a volley of abuse at the officials, he pronounces: 'If someone stops you in a car park and gives you a present, you don't say no, do you?'

Another classic of football ethics. What subconscious Freudian thought processes led Boothroyd to a *car park*? Did it not strike him that some of the 'presents' you get given in car parks need to be handled with care?

As the bickering drags on, and the 'ghost' goal is replayed on every channel, my mind flies back thirty years and I think, Come back, Steve Kember.

Kember, captaining Crystal Palace against Nottingham Forest in the old First Division, was at the centre of an eerily similar controversy at the start of the 1971–2 season. His shot was deflected off a defender, missed the post and went behind for what he assumed was a corner. He was as surprised as anyone when the referee awarded a goal.

'You could see the ball hadn't gone into the net,' he recalls. 'It beats me to this day how the ref missed it.'

What footballer will ever understand referees, those funny little men with rusty whistles and dodgy haircuts? They are two separate species, genetically incompatible, divided by centuries of mutual suspicion.

Kember now coaches football at Whitgift School in Croydon. He is in his sixties, but looks younger, fit as a whippet in his sleek black tracksuit. He played the game with a smile on his face, and the smile is still there. Football is not war by other means: it is meant to be enjoyed.

So what happened after the referee had awarded the non-existent 'goal'?

'Well, the Forest players went berserk, obviously. Peter Hindley, their captain, came up to me and said, "That was never a goal." I said, no, it wasn't a goal, I knew that, but the referee had given it, so there wasn't much I could do. Then, of course, the Forest players go and surround the referee, and I'm thinking, Uh-oh, I know where this is heading.'

Sure enough, seconds later, Kember found himself faced with a sheepish-looking referee muttering, 'Look, I'm in trouble here.' Not in the script. Referees aren't supposed to get into trouble. It's players who get into trouble. The football world was being turned upside down.

'Then he asked me if it had been a goal, I said no, so he gave a goal kick. I said, "Hang about, it wasn't a goal kick, it was a corner", and he said, "I can't change my mind twice." Referees! I ended up feeling quite cheesed off.'

But would he do the same again? 'I suppose so, yes. Mind you, things would be different today. Referees don't talk to players as much as they used to, so I wouldn't be put on the spot in the way I was then. But fair's fair. You have to show some understanding of referees' and their position. They're only human, so they're bound to make mistakes from time to time. It isn't fair to blame them every time they get something wrong.'

Like a surprisingly large number of footballers of his generation, Kember feels lucky to have played when he did. 'We didn't earn anything like as much, obviously, but the game was more honest, played in a better spirit. I can't stand all the diving in the modern game. Football used to be hard but fair: players would kick each other up in the air, then get to their feet and carry on. There wasn't this nonsense of falling over in the penalty area as soon as they're touched. Personally, I'd red-card the worst offenders.'

Among the boys he coaches at Whitgift, scampering across the school playing fields, there could be a David Beckham, a Wayne Rooney, a Theo Walcott. What does he teach them about sportsmanship?

'Well, I don't like them diving, obviously. And I do encourage them to show respect to officials. I wasn't a saint as a player. I was done several times for dissent. But something you learn as you get older is that protesting against decisions is a waste of time. You'll never get a referee to change his mind.'

Except, of course, if you are Steve Kember, who did get a referee to change his mind, and who wrote his own chapter in sporting history by telling the truth, even if it cost his team a goal. It was a brave decision in retrospect.

Asked to explain his actions, Kember has a touchingly straightforward answer. 'I was taught the difference between right and wrong when I was a child. Did you know that my father was a policeman?'

Bobby Pearce: Sport Played with a Smile

EMPICS

Good sportsmanship is not the same as good manners, although the two often get confused, even by people who should know better.

At the Beijing Olympics, Jacques Rogge, President of the International Olympic Committee, publicly criticised the Jamaican sprinter Usain Bolt for the exuberant, fist-pumping way he celebrated his record-breaking wins in the 100m and 200m finals. Rogge took the view that, before showboating, the athlete should have done more to acknowledge the efforts of his fellow competitors. It was a comically prissy response to behaviour which most sports fans recognised for what it was – the spontaneous joy of a man who had just run faster than anyone else in history.

Rogge should have kept his mouth shut or, if he wanted to get on his soap box, directed his ire at his Chinese hosts.

The Beijing games left some golden memories, but a sour aftertaste. The whiff of totalitarian control-freakery was overpowering: it was impossible to escape it. The chicanery of the opening ceremony – with a song sung by a girl with a mouth brace lip-synched by another, more photogenic, girl – was an affront to the whole Olympic family. Now *that* was unsporting – not poor Usain Bolt, thrilling a planet, then daring to celebrate.

Yes, good manners matter in sport, and bad manners are depressing. But there has to be room for raw emotion, the kind that cannot be circumscribed by the canons of polite behaviour. The true sportsman is a competitor first – he has to be, or he would not be there, he would be watching from the stands – and a gentleman second. It is the ongoing tension between those two, sometimes contradictory, demands that animates the underlying human drama. The best sport is not monochrome, but a canvas of many colours.

If sporting brilliance has us up on our feet, whooping and cheering, moments of good sportsmanship affect us in subtler ways. Sometimes they touch us so deeply that we can feel the tears pricking our eyes. Sometimes they are so bold and unexpected that they make the hairs stand up on our necks. More often we simply smile, amused by the sudden gear shift from intense competition to geniality, handshakes and perfect manners. After long hours of edge-of-the-seat tension, we suddenly come down to earth, remember it is only a game and are grateful to the players for reminding us of the fact with the smiles on their own faces.

Winning is not everything and, although spectator sports depend on everyone colluding in the lie that it *is* everything, they also depend on periodic reality checks: reminders that it does not matter, ultimately, whether Arsenal beat Chelsea or Chelsea beat Arsenal. That balance, between two incompatible extremes, can be hard to strike. We have all been to matches where the desire to win has become so all-consuming that the whole atmosphere has turned sour; conversely, we have all been to dreary friendlies where nobody gives a damn what happens, not the players, not the spectators.

The sportsmen who can straddle those two extremes – be passionate or dispassionate, according to the needs of the moment – are the true aristocrats of sport. Bobby Pearce, an Australian sculler between the wars, epitomised the breed.

No film footage, alas, survives of Pearce competing at the 1928 Olympics in Amsterdam, although there is enough biographical detail about him to get a flavour of the man. He came from a sporting family based in Sydney. His father had also been a champion sculler, and he had an aunt and uncle who excelled at swimming and rugby league, respectively. Shades of later Australian sporting dynasties like the Chappells and the Waughs. He was a tall, powerfully built man and, before concentrating on rowing, was a heavyweight boxing champion. He had the DNA of a winner.

Pearce left school early to become a carpenter, a career choice that had unexpected consequences. When he tried to enter the Diamond Sculls at the Henley Royal Regatta in 1928, in preparation for the Amsterdam Olympics, he was rejected out of hand. The snobbishly framed rules debarred anyone 'who is or who has been by trade or employment for wages a mechanic, artisan or labourer'. It was an unhappy introduction to Europe, the kind of setback that makes some sportsmen compete even more fiercely.

Pearce, the only rower from his country selected for the Olympics, carried the Australian flag at the opening cere-mony in Amsterdam. He won his first race by twelve lengths, his second by eight lengths, and was well ahead in his third race, the quarter-final, when . . .

What happened next? Without the history books, we would never guess. A collision? A broken oar? A rules dispute? Nothing so banal.

A family of ducks – five, according to reports – swam across Pearce's lane, right in front of his boat. What was he to do? He had travelled all the way to Europe to compete for his country. He had been snubbed at Henley. He was now confronted by eccentric Dutch stewarding – what were the wildfowl doing on the course? – and would have been well within his rights to send the ducks flying with a mighty swoosh of his oars.

Instead, magnificently, and to the delight of the Dutch crowd, he stopped rowing.

The ducks continued on their way, his French opponent gained a few lengths, then Pearce resumed where he had left off, going on to take the race. After further wins in the semi-final and final, the carpenter from Sydney ended up with the gold medal, confounding the stuffed shirts at Henley. He would win gold again at Los Angeles four years later.

It is not quite a perfect sporting story. If one were tinkering with the script, one would have Pearce lose the race, his gallantry towards his feathered friends costing him precious seconds. That is the fate suffered by many of the sportsmen featured elsewhere in the book. They did the decent thing, paid a heavy price then, paradoxically, earned more laurels for their sportsmanship than they would ever have earned by winning.

But, eighty years on, it is still a touching tale, reflecting the good sporting manners of the time. In the 1920s, with the wounds of the Great War still fresh, there was no danger of sportsmen taking themselves too seriously. For competitors at the Amsterdam Olympics it must have been such fun just to take part that they could afford to be chivalrous.

There is a marvellous story from the same games involving distance runner Paavo Nurmi, the 'Phantom Finn', one of the greatest of all Olympians. In the semi-finals of the steeplechase, Nurmi fell at the water jump and dropped his famous stopwatch – he was one of the first athletes to wear one – in the water. Frenchman Lucien Dusquesne stopped to help the Finn to his feet and find the watch. When they reached the finishing line, with Nurmi leading, the Finn slowed, inviting Dusquesne to pass him and finish first. The Frenchman, matching gallantry with gallantry, declined. After you, Lucien. No, after you, Paavo. Glorious.

Bobby Pearce giving way to ducks exhibited the same quaint courtesy. One can see the whole thing, share the delight of the Dutch crowd, enjoy the sudden gear shift: one minute mayhem, the two men rowing for all they were worth, sweat pouring from their faces; the next serenity and perfect calm, like a sunny afternoon on a suburban boating pond. Olympic gold no longer mattered. Ducks did matter. How stupid. How sublime.

Pete Goss: 'The Biggest Crossroads of My Life'

Round-the-world yachtsman Pete Goss had bigger things than ducks to worry about. If Bobby Pearce belongs to light comedy, Goss is a figure out of *Moby Dick*, man ranged against the unforgiving elements.

His heroics in the 1996 Vendée Globe race, when he battled cold, exhaustion and steepling seas to rescue a French rival off the coast of Australia, made him a national hero twice over, earning him an MBE and the Légion d'honneur, an unprecedented sporting double. When he finally got back to shore in France, there were 150,000 people waiting to greet him. The fact that the rescue took place over Christmas, when other sportsmen were putting their feet up, only gave the story greater exposure. Goss had set out to win the greatest prize in yachting. He had won something far more precious – immortality.

Solo yachtsmen can be a law unto themselves, a cussed, eccentric breed. 'I wouldn't want to be part of one of those big corporate yachting teams where the first member you sign up is a lawyer,' says Goss, when asked about the 1996 Vendée. 'That doesn't press my buttons at all. I'm more interested in adventure. I like the human side of sailing.'

He is a man of iron principle, someone who despises the cheats, the takers of short cuts. 'A bit of dignity doesn't do any harm, does it?' he says of the antics of some of his fellow sportsmen. He comes across as an old-fashioned English romantic, heir to those nineteenth-century explorers who tramped thousands of miles across Africa in searing heat, or set out to the North Pole with a tent and a hip flask, because the challenge excited them. 'One of the sad things that has happened recently,' he says, 'is that people are more interested in trophies than achievements. They want to be photographed on the top of Everest or at the North Pole. But when you look into their stories, half the time you realise that they are just PR stunts. They haven't been to the real North Pole, they've been to the *magnetic* North Pole, which is ten times easier.'

When he reads stories of mountaineers in the Himalayas ignoring other mountaineers in difficulty as they race towards the summit, he is appalled. 'Nothing justifies that sort of behaviour. It's trophy syndrome again.'

For Goss, a down-to-earth son of the West Country who couldn't be pretentious if he tried, there is a right way of doing things and a wrong way. And if you are a round-the-world yachtsman, there is only one way of doing things – the hard way, round the two fearsome capes, the Cape of Good Hope and Cape Horn. 'You can go through the Panama Canal, at a pinch,' jokes Goss, 'but that's the tourist route.' He doesn't do tourism, trophy-bagging: he's an all-or-nothing man.

Born in Devon in 1961, Goss spent most of his child-hood abroad – his father was a consultant in tropical agriculture – then served in the Royal Marines before concentrating on yachting. His participation in the 1996 Vendée Globe, in a boat he had designed himself, was the culmination of ten years of dreaming, planning, making sacrifices, putting family life on hold – in a word, sheer bloody-mindedness, the sort you see in most successful sportsmen.

The Vendée had always been dominated by French yachts-men, so this British upstart, sailing the diminutive *Aqua Quorum*, so amateurish-looking compared with the other boats, was a rank outsider. If he completed the course at all, muttered the cynics, it would be a miracle. But, after an uncertain start, Goss confounded expectations. By the time the boats reached the Southern Ocean he was in the thick of things: off the pace, but gaining on the field. In mid-December he was the fastest boat in the fleet for a full seven days, culminating in a blistering twenty-four-hour run of 344 miles. The dream – not just competing in the Vendée, but winning the bloody thing – was still very much alive.

On 22 December, as Goss celebrated his thirty-fifth birthday, he reflected on how lucky he was. Here he was, ful-filling one of his life's ambitions, doing better in the race than he had dared to hope. There was even a fax from his wife Tracey and his children, saying they had baked a cake and eaten it for him. Goss pampered himself by trimming his moustache and – untold luxury – slipping into a clean set of thermals.

Then, on Christmas Day, with shocking suddenness, the weather intervened – not the kind of squally showers that send cricketers scurrying for the pavilion, but the real McCoy, the gale-force winds and mountainous seas that sailors dread. Goss had been warned by his satellite weather charts – the isobars were so close together that they seemed to merge into a solid black line – but he was unprepared for the ferocity of the storm. 'The wind was a screaming banshee,' he wrote in his autobiography, *Close to the Wind.* 'It lashed the ocean into a frenzy of spume and spray that felt like a shotgun blast on my hands and face.' The wind settled at a vicious fifty knots, but some gusts were nearer sixty.

The *Aqua Quorum* withstood the battering, but, 160 miles to the west, the *Algimouss*, the yacht of Frenchman Raphael Dinelli, was in trouble, after capsizing in heavy seas. Goss received a mayday message and, shortly afterwards, a message from Philippe Jeantot, the race organiser, asking if he could help. It was, he says with feeling, 'a profound moment'.

He couldn't not go to the rescue of the Frenchman. That was the centuries-old tradition of the sea: when someone was in trouble, you helped them. But never mind the danger to himself, having to sail 160 miles into the wind in atrocious conditions. What about the race, and everything he had invested in the race, both financially and emotionally? It was as if ten years of dreams had suddenly been swept overboard, never to be recovered. Even as he altered course, Goss struggled to grasp the enormity of the situation. He had no choice. But what heartache in the choice! And what a terrible price to have to pay for doing the right thing!

Small wonder that, more than ten years later, Goss still refers to that moment of solitary contemplation – the more agonising for being solitary, with nobody else to share his vacillations – as 'the biggest crossroads in my life'. A supreme act of sportsmanship was also a very personal epiphany. 'I knew I had to stand by my morals and principles.'

*

Ghosts from sporting history were swirling around him. Goss was not the first solo yachtsman to have to abandon his race strategy in such circumstances. In the 1984 Transat, the transatlantic equivalent of the Vendée Globe, Frenchman Yvon Fauconnier had to take a sixteen-hour detour to rescue Philippe Jeantot – the same man, ironically, who was now asking Goss to try to rescue Dinelli.

At the 1988 Olympics in Seoul, Canadian yachtsman Lawrence Lemieux rescued not one, but two fellow competitors.

Lemieux was competing in the Finn class, running second in his own event, when he saw two Singaporean sailors in the 470 class in difficulties. A storm had blown up, their boat had overturned and, although it was unclear whether they were in serious danger, the Canadian was not taking any chances. 'I just had to go. If I went to them and they didn't need help, *c'est la vie*. If I didn't go, it would be something I would regret for the rest of my life.'

C'est la vie indeed. One can almost see the Gallic shrug accompanying the words. If model sportsmen have something in common, it is their lack of histrionics. To the world, they are heroes, acting nobly, altruistically. To themselves, they are just doing what comes naturally, accepting the vicissitudes of the sporting life with humour and good grace.

For Lemieux, as for Goss later, the first rule of sailing was that if you saw someone in difficulty you helped them. He duly rescued the two Singaporeans, and although his timing was later adjusted to take account of the time he had lost, he finished fifth in his event, just out of the medals.

'I could have won gold,' the Canadian later reflected. 'But, in the same circumstances, I would do what I did again.'

Lemieux collected a silver medal at the 1990 world championships, but never competed in another Olympics. Thanks to the vagaries of the Korean weather, that dream, the dream of sportsmen the world over, went unfulfilled.

He had to be satisfied with the accolade of the President of the International Olympic Committee, Juan Antonio Samaranch: 'By your sportsmanship, self-sacrifice and courage, you embody all that is right in the Olympic ideal.'

For Pete Goss, battling the elements, thoughts of winning and losing races had dwindled into insignificance. His 160-mile mercy dash through the storm has entered yachting folklore. Simply locating the Frenchman, afloat in a small life raft, was nightmarishly difficult. Goss sailed to where he thought Dinelli *should* be, sent up flare after flare, but got no response. Darkness fell on his efforts, and it was not until the next morning, with the help of an RAAF tracker plane, that Goss found his man. Then it was a question of hauling the Frenchman aboard, his survival suit encrusted with salt and stiff with cold. 'I turned the body over to reveal a nose and two very inflamed eyes surrounded by thick, yellowish wax,' Goss remembers. 'I had no idea that a pair of eyes could convey such a depth of relief and gratitude.'

As the *Aqua Quorum* zigzagged across the Southern Ocean, Goss nursed the Frenchman back to health, before dropping him off in Hobart. The language barrier – as it so often is in sport – was brushed aside as if it did not exist. Pidgin English, with a little help from alcohol, found a way. Four days after his rescue, Dinelli, elated by his escape, faxed his girlfriend to propose to her. She faxed back saying yes and suggesting that Goss be best man at their wedding – an honour he was proud to accept. The two men would later compete together in transatlantic races. In severest adversity, a lifelong friendship had been forged.

As for the Vendée, it had become academic. What was a race compared with this profounder drama of life and death? When Goss finally rejoined the fleet after his detour to Hobart, the race committee allocated him a time allowance in compensation for the time he had spent rescuing Dinelli. But the other boats were too far ahead to be caught. 'I was still keen to finish, but as far as winning was concerned, I had said goodbye to all that. None of it seemed to matter any more: I was too drained, physically and emotionally. Where did I eventually finish? Fifth? Sixth? I couldn't say for sure.'

In the solitude of his yacht, as it completed its journey across the Atlantic, he had little inkling of the celebrity status he had achieved. 'It was like being in a goldfish bowl,' he remembers. 'Other people could see in, but I couldn't see out.' It was only the huge French crowds waiting to greet him that brought home the reality, at once flattering and unsettling, the reality from which he had been cocooned. He was no longer a yachtsman: he was a hero.

A hero but, being an Englishman, with the self-deprecation of the breed, a reluctant hero. You won't hear Pete Goss blowing his own trumpet. All you will hear from him is the philosophical acceptance of sailors through the ages.

'The sea is bigger and more powerful than man will ever be. That's the great tradition of the sea. That's what the Vendée was all about – comradeship and respect between fellow seamen.'

Irene Tidball: The Best Good Sport in Wales

Good sportsmanship does not have to involve life-or-death heroism: in fact, it can sometimes be comically banal. People get called 'good sports' – an old-fashioned term, but an expressive one – for reasons which have nothing to do with their prowess on the sports field.

A player is a good sport if he signs autographs after the match. A referee is a good sport if he falls over on his backside and gets up with a grin on his face. Even spectators can be good sports, turning out in filthy weather to cheer on their team.

I doubt if seventy-two-year-old Welshwoman Irene Tidball has ever played golf, tennis or snooker to professional standard. From the published pictures of her – diminutive, white-haired, bespectacled – she would be hard pushed to run a twenty-minute mile, never mind a four-minute mile. But, beyond question, if there had been a prize for Good Welsh Sport of 2008, Mrs Tidball would have been the runaway winner.

Her son-in-law, Gwilym Rees, is a Welsh football fan who was planning to travel from Cardiff to Moenchengladbach to watch a World Cup qualifying match between Germany and Wales. Unfortunately, Mr Rees cocked up. He thought the supporters' coach was leaving at 1 a.m. on Tuesday morning. In fact, it had already left – at 1 a.m. on Monday morning. Desperately, Mr Rees tried to get a flight to

Germany, found it was too expensive, so decided to drive to the game with his wife, via Dover. There was plenty of time to get to the match. The only problem was that their car did not have the right kind of satnav . . .

One ought really to freeze the action there and ask what sort of geographically challenged football fan has to have a satnav to find a city the size of Moenchengladbach. But that would be to deny Mrs Tidball her fifteen minutes of fame.

Because her car did have a European satnav, and because she had a couple of days free, she offered to drive her daughter and son-in-law all the way to Germany herself. Five hundred miles there, five hundred miles back – with her doing all the driving.

What an incredible sporting journey! One can see the whole thing, as if one is sitting in the car. Mrs T at the wheel, brow furrowed in concentration. Young Gwilym next to her, pinching himself, hardly able to believe his luck. The daughter in the back seat, happy as a sandboy. The disembodied voice of the satnav. ('You are now entering Belgium. Follow signs to Brussels, then take the E314. Continue driving on the right.') A simple trip to a football match has suddenly achieved an epic quality, like something in a movie.

'Talk about the bionic woman,' said an admiring Mr Rees afterwards. 'She's a diamond, she is. When I was telling the boys, they all agreed that their mothers-in-law wouldn't have been as sympathetic.'

I bet they wouldn't. With a single show-stopping gesture, a good Welsh sport had kicked mother-in-law jokes into touch for all time, like a full-back hoofing the ball into Row Z.

'Driving never worries me,' said the indefatigable Mrs Tidball. 'Nothing is too much trouble for those two. They've always been very good to me. I'll do anything for them, short of standing on my head.'

On the pitch, Germany beat Wales 1-0. The Welsh team gave a good account of themselves, according to the reports, but were unable to find the net. Had they lost their satnavs too? Off the pitch, the most unlikely of heroines had hogged the headlines.

Mrs Tidball is obviously a kindly, big-hearted woman. She would probably have done the same if her daughter and son-in-law had been going to Germany to a wedding. But somehow, if it had been a wedding, the story would have had less intrinsic appeal. It is the conjunction of something as trivial as football with a quite heroic act of kindness that stirs the imagination.

It is easy to laugh at the passions which sport inflames, and the way those passions spread and spread, to the point where a septuagenarian Welshwoman starts behaving like Paul Revere on his midnight ride. But the passions are sport. Sometimes they spill over in ugly ways. But they are just as likely to spill over in beautiful ways: reveal the greatness of the human spirit in a flash of unexpected gallantry or generosity.

As Irene Tidball so vividly demonstrated, there is a madness at the heart of sport and, at the heart of that madness, glowing like a flame, is chivalry.

Antilochus, David Beckham and the S-word

EMPICS

A good sport, though, with all due respect to Mrs Tidball, is not quite the same as a good sportsman. The ideals of sportsmanship – always there, at every sporting event, even if only vestigially – have deeper, richer roots.

Sportsmanship as a notion is as old as sport itself. It is impossible to think of one without the other. As soon as the first cavemen could run they must have wanted to run faster than each other, and as soon as they could run faster than each other they must have experienced some vague sense of sporting companionship, a joy in competition that transcended simply winning. *Homo sapiens* knew in his bones that he had to show respect to fellow members of his species. That is what made him *Homo sapiens*.

But what is the first recorded instance of sportsmanship?

Who first demonstrated chivalry in competition? There are a number of candidates but, for me, none fits the bill better than Antilochus, a minor character in Homer's *Iliad*. I first came across him when I was a schoolboy in the 1970s, incarcerated without trial at a boarding school in Somerset, dividing my time between the classroom and the cricket field; and I was immediately enchanted by him.

There will be no other fictional characters in the book. What would be the point of including them? For the writer sitting at his desk, whether he is churning out a Roy of the Rovers comic or a Hollywood screenplay, it is the easiest thing in the world to create a hero who expresses the ideals of chivalry and good sportsmanship. For the real-life sportsman, in the sweat and fury of competition, to act chivalrously towards an opponent is much, much harder – which is why it moves us so much when it happens.

But it would be a shame not to include Antilochus, whose big moment comes in Book XXIII of the *Iliad*. He has as good a claim as anyone to be called the Father of Sportsmanship. He was also, one could plausibly argue, the Father of the Professional Foul.

The *Iliad* dates from the eighth century BC, the same period as the original Olympic Games, which were first held in the year 776. If we want a flavour of what ancient games were like – the sports they featured, the spirit in which they were played – Homer's epic poem makes the perfect starting point. On the windy plains of Troy, beside the wine-dark sea, one can glimpse for the first time a culture of sport and sportsmanship that is still with us. Passion, controversy, spills and thrills, competitors busting a gut to win . . . They are all there, like figures on an Attic vase.

In Book XXIII, the Greek warrior Achilles holds funeral games for his best friend Patroclus, who has been killed in battle. There is boxing and wrestling, archery and discus throwing, and the marquee event, a two-horse chariot race contested by five riders, including Antilochus, son of Nestor.

Antilochus is young and impetuous, bursting with energy and talent, but he has slower horses than his rivals. He is driving a Lotus, not a Ferrari. There is only one way he can win, and that is by using his tactical cunning, stretching the rules to the limit. 'See if you can hit on some artifice to win the prize,' Nestor tells his son, in a pre-race briefing. He advises Antilochus to take the inside track on the bends, driving his rivals out wide.

In the race itself, Antilochus seizes his opportunity when the course suddenly narrows and the chariots have to go single file. In a breach of race etiquette, Antilochus charges recklessly into the gap and forces Menelaus, one of the favourites, to rein back his horses. 'You stupid young fool!' roars Menelaus.

There are no expletives in Homer, or Menelaus would have used one. He is quite Fergusonesque in his outrage and, after the race, launches a furious complaint to the stewards. For a while, the bickering threatens to get out of hand – a useful reminder that, even in Ancient Greece, so often romanticised, athletes were sometimes so desperate to win that they overstepped the bounds of polite behaviour.

And now comes the big moment, the emotional payoff. I remember reading this passage in a Greek translation class and feeling the tears well up in my eyes. It was as good as anything I had read in a football comic.

Antilochus says he is sorry.

'Forgive me,' he says to Menelaus. 'I am younger than you are. You know how easily young men are lured into indiscretion: their tempers are quicker and they have less judgement.' Then he offers to return the prize he has won – a six-year-old breeding mare – rather than lose the friendship of Menelaus or risk incurring the wrath of the gods.

Could there be a more perfect encapsulation of sportsmanship? It is not as if Antilochus has deliberately cheated: he has simply done the chariot-racing equivalent of Lewis Hamilton, or some other pumped-up Formula One driver, trying to overtake on a dangerous corner. He could blag his way out of the situation, tell Menelaus to get lost, insist he was acting within the rules, blame the horses, say it was just one of those things that happen in chariot racing, throw a wobbly, refuse to give interviews, storm out of the room. Instead, calmly and without rancour, he acknowledges he was at fault and acts accordingly.

We must not be sentimental about the Greeks and lazily credit them with spawning 'the Olympic spirit' in the sense that we use the term today. From what we know of the original Olympics, competition could be harsh and uncompromising. Scant respect was shown to losers: they were not honoured, like modern Olympians, simply for taking part. But the Greek mind-set, as illustrated by this little scene from Homer, so characteristic of the *Iliad*, with its cavalcade of noble, larger-than-life heroes, *was* magnanimous. It was underpinned by notions of right and wrong. It was infused with generosity.

Modern professional sportsmen are hewn from the same wood as Antilochus. They are not saints; they are not unfailingly good-mannered; they would not win anything if they were. The best of them lose their temper, overstep the mark, do things they would never do outside the cauldron of competition. Those heat-of-the-moment excesses are part and parcel of professional sport, and we, the paying spectators, accept them as a by-product of the intense physical rivalry which is what brings us through the turnstiles. But the best sportsmen also retain their moral compass. They know when they are out of order, and make swift, generous recompense.

There have been sportsmen who have never behaved badly, never had spats with opponents, never fallen foul of officials. But there have been very few of them and, in nine cases out of ten, their canonisation has been premature: dig deeper into their stories and you find that there have been occasional falls from grace. But, ultimately, they are less interesting than the other kind of good sportsman: the one who is flawed, if only in little ways; whose temper sometimes gets the better of him; but who nevertheless retains an intrinsic sense of right and wrong.

Nothing in David Beckham's career became him better than the unqualified apology he issued after he was sent off against Argentina in the 1998 World Cup, letting a whole nation down with his petulance. Remember that famous headline in the *Daily Mirror* the next day? '10 Heroic Lions, One Stupid Boy'. It was cruel, but it was true.

Beckham could have been gone into denial, grumbled about the referee, tried to shift the blame on to the Argentinian player who had provoked him. That's what a lesser man would have done. That's what many lesser men have done, particularly footballers, for whom using the s-word, saying they are sorry, seems to be an almost physical impossibility, the way it is for some politicians.

But Beckham, beyond the hype, is a decent soul. 'I have apologised to the England players and management,' he said in a statement the next day, 'and I want every English supporter to know how deeply sorry I am.' Simple, clear, word-perfect, with that little 'deeply' performing the same intensifying function as the swerve Beckham puts on his free-kicks.

In apologising so handsomely, when the tabloids were baying for his blood, he showed that he was bigger than his detractors. Yes, he had done something stupid. Many sportsmen, in the heat of the moment, do stupid, graceless, ill-considered things. But, like Homer's Antilochus, he did the manly thing and, without equivocation, said he was sorry.

In football, as Beckham knows better than anyone, it is axiomatic that, if you are taking a penalty or free-kick, you commit to the shot: decide which side of the goalkeeper you are aiming, then strike the ball there with purpose. There is no room for half-measures.

The same also applies to apologies: you have to commit to them or they will sound hollow. One of the banes of modern sport is the half-apology: the statement of 'regret' ringed with so many weasel words, most of them drafted by the club lawyer, that the apologiser is not actually doing what he should be doing, accepting personal responsibility for something he has done wrong. Think of all those spats between rival football clubs which escalate out of control because neither side is willing to give ground until the other side has given ground first.

David Beckham, with his simple s-word, found a better way. He could have been mealy-mouthed, tried to deflect the blame on to someone else; but one suspects that, if he had, his subsequent career might have been different. Self-pity, so often the response of footballers who have been red-carded, might have taken root. It is not a wild exaggeration to say that his status as a global role model had its roots – or some of them – in this moment of contrition in 1998.

If his finest hour on the football field was the last-ditch free-kick against Greece that took England to the 2002 World Cup, his finest moment off it was this gracious, heart-felt apology – a truly Grecian gesture of good sportsmanship which Homer would have applauded.

Patrick Battiston: Forgiving and Forgetting

It takes two to tango, and if a handsome apology is indicative of good sportsmanship, the same applies to the acceptance of an apology. In football, one of the things that has soured the beautiful game is the number of feuds that rumble on for years, with no resolution in sight. Grown men throw their toys out of the pram and vow never to talk to each other again. There is vindictiveness where there should be reconciliation. When Roy Keane infamously hacked down Alf-Inge Haaland, in retaliation for past wrongs, it was more like a scene from *The Godfather* than a Premiership football match.

What was the spat between Sir Alex Ferguson and the BBC about? It happened so long ago that the rest of us have forgotten. But still, bizarrely, our greatest football manager refuses to give interviews to our national broadcaster.

In football, irksomely, it is often the people in positions of leadership who are the least forgiving. In 2008, when Scotland played Argentina in a friendly, the assistant Scotland manager Terry Butcher refused to shake hands with the Argentina manager Diego Maradona. Butcher, a former England player, had not yet forgiven Maradona for the infamous 'Hand of God' goal that knocked England out of the 1986 World Cup – twenty-two years earlier. Rank-and-file England football fans were much quicker to forgive and forget. In a 2002 TV poll of the Hundred Greatest British Sporting Moments, the second goal Maradona scored in that match, one of the most brilliant in footballing history, was voted sixth – ahead of any goal ever scored by an Englishman.

Another lesson in the art of forgiveness was provided by the French defender Patrick Battiston.

Battiston was a fine player and earned more than fifty caps for his country, but the episode for which he is best remembered, in the semi-final of the 1982 World Cup in Spain, does not feature his footballing skills.

The semi-final pitched France against West Germany in Seville. The game was tied at 1-1 in the second half when Battiston, who had come on as a substitute, was put through on goal by a defence-splitting pass by Michel Platini. Glory beckoned for the Frenchman, but the German goalkeeper, Harald 'Toni' Schumacher, had other ideas, flattening Battiston with a reckless head-high challenge, one of the most X-rated tackles ever seen at the World Cup. The Dutch referee, to general disbelief, took no action.

As Battiston lay unconscious on the ground, he was so pale that Platini thought he was dead. He had lost three teeth and had to be given oxygen before being stretchered from the field. Schumacher kept his distance. He later explained, rather feebly, that he did not go and check up on the Frenchman because the other French players were standing around Battiston, making threatening gestures in his direction. His whole demeanour seemed unrepentant. After the game, when told about the teeth Battiston had lost, he snapped to reporters: 'If that's all that's wrong with him, I'll pay for the crowns.' Stretching credulity, he insisted that he had not deliberately impeded Battiston: it had just been an accidental clash of bodies.

The footballing gods – who, it has to be said, are not as assiduous or fair-minded as their counterparts in other sports – were particularly unfeeling that day. While Battiston was being rushed to hospital, his German assailant, instead of being sent off, became the hero of the hour. The game went to extra time, then penalties, and it was Schumacher's brilliant saves in the shoot-out that took the Germans through to the final.

It was one of the grossest injustices in World Cup history, the kind that sets nation against nation and threatens to spill over on to the streets. When a French newspaper asked readers who was the most unpopular man in France, Schumacher topped the poll, with Adolf Hitler runner-up. Anger at the tackle itself was fuelled by an apparent lack of contrition from the German camp.

But there was to be a happy ending – or as happy an ending as was possible in the circumstances.

West Germany were well beaten by Italy in the final, so the ultimate injustice was averted. Schumacher, seeing sense at last, offered to visit Battiston and apologise in person. And the Frenchman, to his eternal credit, accepted the offer. The hatchet was buried within days.

In the collective memory of football fans, encyclopaedic in their recall of past wrongs, The Horror Tackle That the

Referee Missed still lingers on. But at a human level, thanks to one man's magnanimity, the boil had been lanced. When West Germany and France, by a strange coincidence, found themselves contesting the semi-final of the next World Cup, in Mexico, Battiston told reporters before the match that the Seville incident had been 'forgiven and forgotten'.

He did add, wryly, that he did not intend to go within forty yards of the German goalkeeper. Professional footballers are professional footballers: there are limits to their magnanimity.

It's Not the Winning . . .

'It's not the winning that counts, it's the taking part.'

For Englishmen of my generation the words were as much a part of childhood as jam roly-poly or conker fights. They entered our lives when we were very young. They were the cliché of choice of a thousand games masters. They were offered in consolation after sporting disappointments – a duck at cricket or a thrashing at football – and they *did* provide consolation. We remembered them. We filed them away among the bits and pieces of folklore we would one day pass on to our own children. And there they stayed, in their little pigeon-hole, next to that other classic of English humbug – 'the Battle of Waterloo was won on the playing fields of Eton'. That one felt good, too, particularly on a cold day, with the rain starting to fall, and the wind howling across the pitch, when winning an under-eleven football match was in danger of losing its urgency.

Journeyman English boxer Peter Buckley did not go to Eton and, judging by an interview he gave in *Boxing Monthly* in 2005, avuncular games masters offering words of consolation played little or no part in his childhood.

'When I was fifteen, me dad passed on and I really went off the rails. They chucked me out of school for fighting and I was sent to special school. I started robbing cars, robbing shops, fighting, being violent and, at fifteen, I was locked up. I came out fit as fuck, started training but ended up back out robbing, locked up again. Vicious cycle, man.'

It is a sorry tale, without redeeming features. But Birmingham-born Buckley did achieve redemption, and he achieved it through sport – not by winning, but by taking part, again and again and again.

When he went into the ring against Matin Mohammed on 31 October 2008, it was his three hundredth profes-sional fight, an all-time British record. Of the previous 299, he had won just 31, with 12 draws. At the age of thirty-nine, the bumbling super-featherweight had become little better than a human punch-bag, having failed to win in eighty-eight successive bouts. When he announced that the fight against Mohammed would be his last, there were sighs of relief throughout the boxing world. His last victory had been in 2003. He should have thrown in the towel years ago.

A commission in the United States recently recom-mended that boxers who lost ten consecutive bouts should forgo their licences. It sounds like a sensible suggestion, striking a fair balance between the freedom of boxers to practise their trade and the supervisory responsibilities of boxing boards of control. But there were no such restraints on Buckley. He just went on losing, month after month, year after year. He lost so often that he sometimes turned up in the ring with a black eye from his previous fight.

From a medical point of view his boxing philosophy was frighteningly simplistic. 'If you phone up a bricklayer and ask him to build you a wall, he doesn't ask for three weeks to prepare. He comes round and does it straight away. Why should a boxer be any different?'

To equate what must seem like pure masochism with sportsmanship will probably strike some people as perverse, even irresponsible. But the important thing to remember about Buckley is that he did not *choose* defeat. Every time he went into the ring – and he faced some formidable opponents in his time, including Duke McKenzie, Prince Naseem Hamed and other world champions – he nursed hopes of winning. He did not lightly or wantonly invite further punishment. He was a natural-born optimist who just happened to lose a lot.

The serial loser, *per se*, is a figure of no interest. But when sporting incompetence is allied to physical courage, the equation changes. If Eddie the Eagle, the memorably awful British ski-jumper of the 1980s, had been, say, a table-tennis player, his antics would have attracted little attention. It was the fact that he looked likely to break a leg every time he landed that kept us hypnotised. Peter Buckley, returning gamely to the ring when everyone else had written him off, stirred the imagination for the same reason.

In that 2005 interview, as Buckley recalls his triumphs and disasters, you cannot miss the note of irrepressibility, the bulldog spirit. 'I knocked him sparko, but me shoulder's totally fucked . . . carried on fighting one-armed . . . ninth round, I creamed him with a body shot, clipped him on the way down and he's out, man . . . never had a scratch on me . . . sometimes have a bad day at the office and box shit . . . just grit me teeth . . . it's only the world-class geezers that have stopped me.'

The critics of boxing are not going to go away, nor should they. It is a barbaric sport. But if there is such a thing as a good advertisement for boxing, then it is Buckley. You fear for any boxer when he goes into the ring against a superior opponent. But it is also possible, without being unduly sentimental, to fear for a boxer deprived of the dignity which his profession confers on him.

Take boxing out of the life of Peter Buckley and what are you left with? Perhaps the boxer himself should be allowed to answer that question: 'The boxing's allowed me to have nice holidays. I've got a nice home. I drive a nice car and me daughter and me missus have nice things. But it really ain't just about the money. Boxing kept me out of prison, tell you the truth. Me brother Johnny, who's dead now, was in and out of jail. One of me nephews is doing eleven years, another's doing eight for robbing vans. Loads of other mates are inside. Today, I hang around in different circles, do me own thing. The game has allowed me to earn a lot of respect and it's increased me own self-respect. I've won several awards for services to boxing. Me old mum, who's sixty-eight now, keeps 'em all.'

As for sportsmanship, you will never find it more simply or eloquently described.

'I've never disrespected anyone I've fought and I've never disliked any of my opponents either. Afterwards I pop into their changing room or they come to mine and we'll have a cup of tea together. I wish 'em all the best and I genuinely mean it. They're just trying to earn a few quid like me.'

How many serial winners have shown such an exemplary attitude?

Sporting morality tales, like sport itself, keep you guessing to the very last minute. If Buckley had lost his farewell fight and, in the process, done himself lasting physical damage, the story of a never-say-die fighter would have assumed a much darker hue. As it was, his swansong, cheered on by the Birmingham faithful, exceeded all expectations.

He not only got out of the ring in one piece, but actually beat his opponent, on a points decision – his first victory in five years.

'I definitely won't miss being punched in the face for a living,' he joked afterwards, as he accepted the plaudits of the crowd. Then it was back to the dressing room for one final cuppa with his opponent. A sporting life of epic under-achievement had ended on the perfect note.

The Emperor Titus and the First Score Draw

If the Greeks gave birth to ideals of fair sporting competition that endure to this day, the Romans had a much harsher philosophy. There was not much room for gallantry in a Roman amphitheatre: if you got out alive, you counted yourself lucky.

But even in Ancient Rome there were grace notes, little moments of humanity when the blood lust of the crowd suddenly abated. One of the most notable instances was provided by the Emperor Titus, who reigned from AD 79 to 81. He probably seems wildly out of place in a book about modern sport, but, as with Homer's Antilochus, furnishes telling insights into sporting attitudes at a time when sport was in its infancy. Notions of sportsmanship did not suddenly come into being in the nineteenth century, when W. G. Grace was growing his first beard and the rules of the various sports were being codified. They have much deeper roots.

Titus only ruled for two years and his reign got off to a calamitous start. Vesuvius erupted almost as soon as he took power. Rome was struck by plague and fire the following year. But he has passed into history and folklore as a model of compassion. In Mozart's opera *La Clemenza di Tito*, he is positively swilling with magnanimity, sparing his enemies right, left and centre. Good-looking, too, according to the historians.

He also made a modest contribution to the development of sport. The Flavian Amphitheatre, the modern Colosseum, was opened during his reign. Hollywood has hopelessly distorted the world of Roman gladiators and, as with the ancient Olympic Games, half of what we think we know about what went on in the Colosseum is myth, pure and simple. There is no evidence, for example, for the enduring popular conception that the Emperor gave a thumbs-up if a gladiator was to be spared, a thumbs-down if he was to be killed. Something went on with thumbs; but quite what is debated. There is one theory that a fist raised with the thumb compressed inside it was a symbolic plea for mercy. A small lake of scholarly ink has been expended on the subject.

There were plenty of fights to the death, of course, and many losing gladiators paid the ultimate price. Crowds were large, raucous and bloodthirsty. Public executions were routinely held between gladiatorial bouts. Slaves, wild animals, prisoners of war, even prostitutes, were all conscripted into the dance of death. But there also seems to have been room for chivalry and good sportsmanship. Both qualities are in evidence in one of the few gladiatorial encounters of which we have a contemporary account – the epic showdown between Priscus and Verus described by the poet Martial in his *Liber de Spectaculis.*

Priscus and Verus were two of the leading gladiators of the day, and their fight, in front of the Emperor Titus, was the highlight of the games held to celebrate the opening of the Colosseum. It would have been, at least potentially, a fight to the death, with the prize for the winner decided on an ad hoc basis. Common prizes included a laurel crown, some gold coins or, most treasured of all, a wooden sword, which traditionally symbolised the releasing of the gladiator from the obligation to fight.

On this occasion, according to Martial, the two gladiators fought so evenly and so bravely for so long, with the crowd baying for a winner, that they eventually conceded defeat at the same time, each man raising his finger in the traditional gesture of surrender.

At this point Titus, instead of insisting, as more sadistic Emperors would have done, on a fight to the finish, awarded victory to both men, giving each of them a laurel crown and a wooden sword. What a man! Two thousand years on, the simple humanity of the gesture, in the frenzied surroundings of the Colosseum, still has the power to touch. Titus was Emperor: he could do what he wanted. But, from the admiring way Martial describes the episode, he was doing something quite out of the ordinary: confounding the expectations of the crowd; chucking out the rule book; finding an imaginative, humane solution to an unforeseen situation

As Martial puts it, '*Cum duo pugnarent, victor uterque fuit.*' 'Two men fought each other, but both were the winners.' If he had known he was giving birth to one of the most tiresome clichés in sport – 'The game of football/cricket/rugby was the winner' – he would probably have found a better way of putting it. But, of course, he was right, as the Emperor Titus was right.

It isn't compulsory to have a single winner. Sometimes the deepest needs of sport are served by a recognition that nothing, ultimately, separates the competitors: they are equal in value; equal in dignity; equal in the place they have in our affections and loyalties.

When the London Marathon was first run, in 1981, it ended in a dead heat – not because the first two men home could not be separated by the stopwatch, but because they chose to finish together, hand in hand. Inge Simonsen of Sweden and Dick Beardsley of the United States wrote their own chapter in sporting history, bearing witness to the spirit of comradeship – shared endeavour, shared exhaustion – that is the heartbeat of a big-city marathon.

It was a wonderful moment, and it is sad that it has been so seldom replicated since, sad that the winner-takes-all ethos has taken such a stranglehold on sport.

As Roger Federer and Rafael Nadal battled each other to a standstill in the 2008 men's singles final at Wimbledon, with the light fading on their heroics, I can remember thinking, and I am sure I was not alone, Does this marvellous match have to have a winner?

It was 7-7 in the fifth set, with nothing to separate the two players, and by the time it got to 10-10 or 11-11, the way things were going, they would be playing in pitch darkness. After nearly five hours of high drama, bathos beckoned: the anti-climax of a stoppage for bad light, followed by ten minutes of tennis the next morning, with the Centre Court half empty. Would it not be more fitting, if it got to that point, to let the two men – titans of their sport – share the spoils?

The statisticians wouldn't have liked it: they like their

facts and figures cut and dried. Probably the players would-
n't have liked it either. They were playing for colossal stakes:
Nadal for his first Wimbledon title; Federer for his sixth
title in a row, beating Bjorn Borg's record. But, emotionally – as various hypothetical scenarios scuttled through my
head – the idea of an honourable draw appealed more than
a messy, delayed victory.

Mercifully, Nadal rendered my conundrum academic,
beating Federer in the nick of time, then receiving the
trophy in near-darkness, lit up by the flashbulbs, all teeth
and ears, like a rabbit caught in a car headlights. And fifteen
thousand fans stumbled home, drunk with joy at what they
had seen.

But the original question still stands. Does there always
have to be a winner in sport? Aren't there times, more times
than there already are, when honours should be declared
even? Some of the most fondly remembered of all sporting
encounters – like the famous Tied Test in Brisbane in 1960 –
failed to deliver an outright winner. Yet still sports administrators, through force of habit, insist on a single champion,
a single cup-holder, even if it requires totally unsatisfactory
tie-breakers, like the penalty shoot-out in football, to produce one.

It takes courage, imagination, a touch of genius, to challenge that way of thinking.

Step forward, John Francome.

John Francome: Sharing the Spoils

For the perpetrator of one of the all-time great sporting gestures, Francome is remarkably vague about the details. 'Nineteen eighty-two? Was that when it was? Are you sure it wasn't 1983? It all happened such a long time ago.'

Not all successful sportsmen are happy in retirement: they miss the glory days; they are nagged by what-ifs and might-have-beens; they feel the encroachment of old age more keenly than people who have been flabby and muscle-bound since they were teenagers.

But Francome, seven times winner of the National Hunt Jockeys' Championship, is the exception that proves the rule. Since retiring from riding, he has enjoyed further success, both as a bestselling novelist and as a commentator on Channel 4. Life has been kind to him, and he knows it, and he is more impressive as a human being because of that.

Sportsmen are often most revealing when they choose a title for their autobiography. Francome's – *Born Lucky* – says all you need to know about the man. An achiever, but a humble achiever, the sort who has to pinch himself from time to time to make sure it is not all a dream.

In a profession dominated by Irish jockeys, Francome, the son of a Swindon railwayman, is a colourful oddball. His parents had wanted him to be a vet, but by the time he left school – in 'a rough part of town, where even the Alsatians go round in pairs' – he had only two pieces of pink paper to his name: one stating that he had obtained a low pass in metalwork, the other that he had managed an even lower one in geography. Luckily, he had also acquired a passion for horses, progressing from gymkhanas to show-jumping before getting involved in racing.

Francome is fifty-six but looks younger, his fitness honed by five-a-side indoor football, and by golf, another of his passions. Sitting in the kitchen of his Berkshire farmhouse, overlooking the downs where generations of jockeys have ridden out for their morning gallop, he seems mildly embarrassed when questioned about 1982 – it was 1982, not 1983 – the year when he astonished the racing world by deliberately not winning a coveted prize.

The Jockeys' Championship – it would have been his fourth – was there for the taking, but decency, kindness, soft-heartedness, a crisis of conscience, call it what you will, held him back.

What happened exactly?

Francome looks sheepish, as if he has been accused of cheating. Cheating? He is about to tell one of the most honourable stories in modern sport, the kind that puts cheats to shame.

'I just felt sorry for Peter Scudamore,' he explains. His

younger rival was coming up through the ranks, but seemed to be jinxed by bad luck. The previous year, Scudamore would probably have won the championship, but broke his leg in a fall, so Francome won it instead. Then, in 1982, history repeated itself. Scudamore was well out in front – about twenty winners ahead of Francome – when he broke his arm in another fall, at Southwell. 'You started to wonder if he was one of those unlucky jockeys who never win anything because Fate is against them.'

What happened next was so jaw-droppingly gallant, so far removed from the ethos of modern professional sport, that it seems to belong to the world of the medieval joust. While Scudamore was still recovering in hospital, Francome rang up Scudamore's father and told him of his extraordinary decision: he would continue riding until he had got the same number of winners as Scudamore, 120, then stop for the season, so that the two men could share the championship.

'I think I had been 6/4 to win the championship before Peter had his fall,' he remembers. 'So there may have been a few punters lost out. But I didn't mind about them.'

True to his promise, Francome caught up with Scudamore in the championship race, riding his 120th winner at Uttoxeter, then called it a day for the season. The trophy – fittingly, as more and more people were beginning to see – was shared.

'With hindsight,' Francome concedes, 'if I had known that Peter would go on and win the title another seven times, and ride far more winners in his career than me, I would never have done it. But I couldn't know that, could I? If I had my time again, I'd do exactly the same thing. Sport, for me, is not about some desperate desire to win: it is more about not wanting to lose, not having to settle for second. Does that make sense?'

He and Scudamore now play golf together regularly, but back in 1982 were not particularly close friends – which makes Francome's gesture of renunciation all the more remarkable.

'Some things are just *right*,' he says stubbornly, insistent that he deserves no credit for what he did. 'If you've been brought up the right way, you know what you need to do in these situations.' He contributes a lot of his native good humour to his father, a jolly, uncomplaining soul whose two favourite sayings were 'Make work a pleasure' and 'If all else fails, read the instructions'.

The tone is wry, modest, matter-of-fact. The cleverest cross-examiner in the world could not get Francome to admit that he did something exceptional, glorious, tinged with nobility. But that does not make him an innocent, a holy fool, someone who acts without thinking. Get him started on the theme of sportsmanship in general, and the spark of passion ignites.

'People say it's impossible to be competitive, and win things, and still play the game in the right spirit. That's utter rubbish. Being a professional sportsman is no excuse for not behaving properly. You look at all those footballers claiming throw-ins when they know it's not their throw. Can't they see how ridiculous they look? Sportsmen are remembered for how they behave.'

In racing circles, Francome is known as an iconoclast, someone not afraid to speak his mind. He has relished challenging some of the archaic traditions of a notoriously class-ridden sport. As a young jockey he was once summoned before the stewards at Kempton with the words, 'Francome, we want you.' 'I'm not going anywhere,' he retorted, 'until you call me John or Mr Francome.' He got his way. As a no-nonsense commentator, he has made enemies as well as friends.

But, thanks to the events of 1982, he has secured a distinctive niche in sporting history: a supremely generous sharer in a world of me-first grabbers. The pursuit of victory, the mainspring of all sport, needs as its corollary the willingness, occasionally, to abandon the chase and set aside thoughts of winning. Perspective – the ability to step back and see life whole, not through the distorting lens of competition – is all.

Or, in John Francome's own words, ripe with West Country common sense, 'When you're doing something you enjoy with a load of lads you get on with, you should count yourself lucky – winning is just a bonus.'

Renouncing the sweets of victory is so intrinsically noble, good sportsmanship at its most heart-warming, that perhaps one should also salute a sensational act of renunciation which made front-page news in November 2008. *Strictly Come Dancing* belongs at the very outer fringes of sport, if not beyond them, but the comically bad performances of the former BBC political correspondent John Sergeant had millions on the edge of their seats.

Sixty-four-year-old Sergeant may have murdered the foxtrot and the *paso doble*, but exuded such geniality and warmth that, the more the expert judges sneered at his efforts, the more the voting public took him to their hearts. Week after week, they evicted other celebrities – and far superior dancers – instead of Sergeant. The possibility of the man with two left feet winning the whole show loomed larger and larger – to the point that a *Times* leader rubbed its hands at the possibility, applauding the

Sergeant bandwagon as a fine example of democracy in action.

Sergeant had to endure so many cheap shots from the judges, who were aghast that such an inept dancer should be so popular with the public, that it would have been only human to want to milk that popularity. Instead, he graciously withdrew from the contest, saying: 'I only entered the show to have fun, but there was now a real danger that I might win it – which would have been a joke too far.'

It was a magnificent – one could almost say Francome-esque – gesture.

The Corinthians: When Not to Play to the Whistle

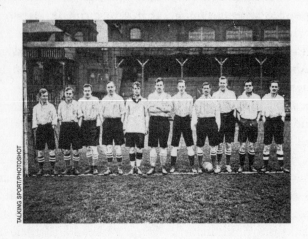

No history of sportsmanship would be complete without reference to the famous Corinthian Football Club, those fine exemplars of English amateurism. The story of the Corinthians has been told many times, most recently by Rob Cavallini in his absorbing *Play Up Corinth*, published in 2007. Reading the book in the twenty-first century is a surreal experience. Some of the score lines are mind-boggling. Just take this one from the 1904–5 season. Corinthians 11, Manchester United 3. Even Arsenal- or Liverpool-obsessed schoolboys only thrash United by *ten* goals in their nocturnal fantasies.

From the inception of the club, in 1882, moral integrity was in the Corinthians' bloodstream. Here they are playing Aston Villa in the 1892–3 season:

. . . a peculiar incident occurred. Sandilands took rapidly down the wing and kicked across to Gosling. The Old Etonian shot obliquely and the ball landed within the goal net. The referee returned to midfield under the impression that the Corinthians had drawn level. Roberts, however, claimed that the ball had broken through the side of the net, and Gosling and Cotterill, in sportsmanlike fashion, upheld this view, the official being reluctantly induced to return and examine the net, when he found the claim justified and disallowed the item.

Yes, I think one can call that a peculiar incident. By modern standards – and we have already seen what happened after a similar incident in the Watford–Reading match – it is a *very* peculiar incident. But how can you not applaud the Corinthian players involved? Note, incidentally, the reluctance of the referee to reverse his decision. Give a man a whistle and, nine times out of ten, he becomes a self-important fool. But the Corinthian does not let that self-importance ruin the game. He has his own unerring moral compass.

In their heyday, before the Great War, the Corinthians not only played highly entertaining football but embarked on a series of overseas tours whose impact was incalculable. Would football even have taken off in countries like Germany and Brazil if it had not been played with such panache by those moustachioed figures in baggy shorts or, as they knew them, baggy knickers?

Wherever the Corinthians went, they won hearts and minds. They were playing for pleasure, not money, and that pleasure communicated itself to spectators. People liked what they saw and wanted to emulate it. Real Madrid, famously, adopted the Corinthians' white shirt in their honour. Other clubs took their name. Long before Pele coined the phrase 'the beautiful game', the Corinthians were garnering the kind of reviews you would expect to see on the arts pages.

'The tactical subtleties of the game were carried out in worthy, clean, sporting and almost youthful joy, dainties indeed for the connoisseur,' wrote a star-struck Swiss reporter, after watching a Corinthians game in Berne. 'The charming football minuets and two-steps were worthy of the brush of Watteau, the most beautiful Rococo from the best drawing-room of the finest football aristocracy.' Through the fog of mixed metaphors, painting and music colliding like defenders going for the same ball, a whole sporting aesthetic can be glimpsed.

The men in those old black-and-white photographs, hands stuffed deep into their trouser pockets, or puffing at pipes, may look like Monty Python characters, but they were true sporting missionaries, with sportsmanship intrinsic to their mission. The most celebrated instance of this was their attitude to penalties.

Today's football fan takes penalty kicks entirely for granted. Any controversy only arises when the award or non-award of a penalty is disputed. The Corinthians looked more deeply into the subject, and what they saw, although it may seem like the wildest of hallucinations, is worth reflecting on.

To the Corinthian mind, the idea of awarding a penalty kick for deliberate foul play had a fatal flaw: it pre-supposed that a gentleman playing football was *capable* of deliberate foul play. A game was a game: to cheat to gain an advantage contravened the essence of sport.

When penalties were first introduced in 1891, the

Corinthians took very strong exception. Their objections were colourfully summed up by one of the most celebrated of all Corinthians, C. B. Fry, the pre-eminent all-round sportsman of his age, better known as a cricketer. How, Fry demanded, could Corinthians be expected to respect a rule which presumed that players could 'trip, hack and kick their opponents and behave like cads of the most unscrupulous kidney'?

For Fry, the new rule introduced the principle that 'if there is a penalty for cheating, then it is permissible to cheat at the expense of a penalty'. And where did that leave football? 'It is now widely acknowledged,' he wrote, in words that ring with the force of prophecy, 'that if both sides agree to cheat, cheating is fair.' And they had not even invented diving in 1891.

In popular folklore, the Corinthians refused to have anything to do with the new rule: if a penalty was awarded in their favour, they would deliberately miss it; if it was awarded against them, the Corinthian goalkeeper would stand aside and let the opposition score. Brilliant! You cannot fault the moral logic of their position in any way: it is as intellectually elegant as a proposition by Aristotle or Wittgenstein. Sadly, there is no evidence of them putting their precepts into practice on a regular basis: just the odd isolated episode, fondly remembered.

It is hard to listen to this account of the Corinthians' 1907 tour of South Africa by Old Etonian Henry Hugh-Onslow – not a name you would expect to find on an Arsenal or Chelsea team sheet – without a smile of pure happiness:

When the Corinthian team went to play in South Africa, the penalty kick had been in force long

enough to satisfy us that it was calculated to engender
a spirit very unlike that in which we intend to play
the game. The Corinthians were determined to do all
in their power to show that the game could be played
in such a spirit that the referee would never be
allowed to interfere on the ground of foul play.
Accordingly, very early in the tour, if not in the first
match, when it happened that the referee awarded a
penalty kick in favour of the home side, the
Corinthian captain immediately explained to his
opponents that, although in the opinion of the
referee a member of his side had been guilty of foul
play, the Corinthians had no wish to prevent their
opponents scoring by any such means, and he
accordingly ordered his goalkeeper to stand clear of
the goal and offer no opposition to the goal being
scored. Not long afterwards, the converse case
occurred: a penalty kick being awarded to the
Corinthians for something which, in their opinion,
certainly did not amount to deliberate foul play.
Thereupon the Corinthian captain, taking the kick
himself, made no attempt to score a goal, but sent the
ball off the ground over the touch line. I need hardly
mention the effect that this, to my mind, admirably
conceived action had upon the spirit in which the
subsequent matches were played, but if you can
believe it, the Council of the Football Association
seriously debated the question of whether or not the
Corinthians should be called to explain their
unsportsmanlike conduct.

It is a gorgeous story, and it is worth noting not just the
obvious moral – the Football Association are idiots and

always have been – but the lesser, secondary moral – referees can be overruled. As with that disallowed goal in the Aston Villa match, the Corinthians did not play to the whistle willy-nilly, but applied their own, higher, morality.

A common misconception about sportsmanship is that the true sportsman respects the rulings of officials at all times. Wrong. Sometimes officials, being only human, make such glaring mistakes, or perpetrate such rank injustices, that their decisions need to be challenged. It is the players, and the bonds of respect between them, that constitute true sport: the man with the whistle is just an accessory.

That fine amateur sportsman Arthur Conan Doyle, who spent a fair chunk of his life fighting injustices, showed just what he thought of over-zealous officials at the 1908 Olympics in London. The *cause célèbre* of the games was the disqualification of the Italian marathon runner Dorando Pietri, who entered the stadium in the lead, but then started staggering about like a punch-drunk boxer. Onlookers – including Conan Doyle himself, according to some accounts – came to his aid and helped him across the line, cheered on by the crowd. The official explanation of his disqualification, that Pietri had 'used external support', seems not unreasonable, in retrospect. But it outraged Conan Doyle, who leapt to the Italian's defence.

Having reported on the games for the *Daily Mail*, he launched an appeal in the paper for a fund to honour the athlete for his gallantry. 'No Roman of prime had ever borne himself better; the great breed is not extinct.' A few days later, a small crowd gathered in the newspaper's offices, where Conan Doyle's wife Jean presented Pietri with a cheque for £308 10s and a gold cigarette case, while Arthur commended his sportsmanship on behalf of 'all the English nation'.

As he saw it, the officials had been cack-handed, the way the police sometimes are in the Sherlock Holmes stories; they had applied the letter, not the spirit, of the law. And just as the great detective, on occasion, takes the law into his own hands, so Conan Doyle took it on himself to deliver sporting justice. It was a Corinthian episode in every sense.

As for the Corinthians themselves, their days were sadly numbered. Even before the Great War, they were struggling to compete with the best professional teams; after it, they were outplayed right across the pitch. Their amateurism was by now painfully obvious. In 1919, when they lost 4-0 to Tottenham Hotspur, they started the game with only nine players, like a pub side. In 1924, during a 5-0 drubbing by West Bromwich Albion, they stopped playing when an opposition player was injured, waiting for a whistle that never came. In 1932, as they celebrated their fiftieth anniversary, they held a big dinner at the Dorchester, before playing Arsenal the next day, the worse for wear. They were hammered 9-2.

'The atmosphere resembled a memorial service rather than a parade of soccer talent,' wrote an observer at a thinly attended match at White City in 1937, when the Corinthians took their last bow in the FA Cup, beaten 2-0 by Southend United. 'The occasional whisper of "Play up Corinth" filtered through the murky air like some haunting cry that one snatches to retain but always slides away.'

In 1939, with another war looming, the Corinthians merged with another amateur club, the Casuals. The Corinthian adventure was at an end, although their legacy, unquestionably, endures.

England football – and one could say the same of England in general – is always looking wistfully back over its shoulder. Will we ever recapture the happiness we felt on that never-to-be-forgotten July day in 1966, when Bobby Moore lifted the World Cup and a whole nation danced in the streets? The past seems more glorious than the present. Things were better then – whenever then was. And a lot of that regret for a lost Eden centres on those baggy-shorted pioneers, playing the game with an uncomplicated joy that seems poignantly irretrievable.

Sport can take itself too seriously, and often does; but the importance of sport as an arena for idealism, a moral testing ground, can hardly be overstated. In 1922, when a memorial was unveiled to the Corinthians who lost their lives in the Great War, with a commemorative match scheduled for after the ceremony, the headmaster of Winchester, Dr M. J. Rendall, a former Corinthian, made the point very powerfully in his address:

> There is no clash or contradiction between our eager
> expectancy and our solemn remembrance: between
> the game of five minutes hence and the battle of five
> years ago. The one is the prelude of the other. Both
> are rooted in honour, in courage, in chivalry.
>   Matches like this are tournaments; athletes are
> knights of chivalry; and as tournaments had at first
> no meaning except as a training for a Crusader's life,
> so your matches, played in the spirit of chivalry, have
> no lower aim. They are a stage in training for
> Christian service. You make yourself strong that you
> may serve your generation.

Wherever football is played, however cynically, however rancorously, Corinthian ideals are there in the background, like honours boards on the changing-room wall. Paradoxically, the team doomed to redundancy has become a timeless icon of fair play.

Fair Play, Shakespeare and the Marathon Runner of Venice

PA PHOTOS

Fair play. We take the phrase for granted. It is intrinsic to what we mean by sport. We look for it in our sporting heroes and heroines. We mourn its absence when it goes missing. But the phrase itself is not as venerable as you might think. 'Foul play' entered the language earlier.

It is an English expression and to an extent, an English concept. Modern professional footballers hop frog-like from Berlin to Barcelona, from Milan to Moscow. Language does not travel quite so easily.

'Fair play is a great conception,' wrote an admiring German visitor to England in the 1920s. 'In these two words are summed up all that English education and ethics hold most dear. But the words are untranslatable, and it would be an injustice to cramp them into a rough and ready formula . . . Everyone, be he sportsman, politician, statesman, journalist, finds in these two words guidance and admonishment ... Fair play means regard for one's neighbour and seeing the man and fellow player in one's opponent.'

The German for 'fair play' – and the same is true of French, Japanese and many other languages – is 'fair play'. There's nothing wrong with that. When we want to describe the glee an English football fan feels when a German misses a penalty, we resort to the German expression *Schadenfreude*. But it hints at subtle cultural differences.

Would Jürgen Klinsmann, say, have fallen over quite so easily in the opposition penalty area if he had been brought up in Yorkshire, learning about fair play on his mother's knee? One could pose the same question in relation to Maradona and that infamous 'Hand of God' goal. The closest Spanish equivalent to 'fair play' is '*juego limpio*', where the '*limpio*' denotes cleanliness, as in teeth that have just been brushed or bathroom floors that have just been scrubbed. The phrase has none of the associative richness of 'fair play'. You don't feel conscience-struck because you've forgotten to clean the bathroom.

Even English-speaking countries, curiously, have been reluctant to adopt the expression. By the time it gets off the plane in Sydney, 'fair play' has become 'fair dinkum'. The phrase is nearly synonymous, but not quite. The fair-dinkum Aussie slip fielder has no qualms about sledging which, to the Anglo-Saxon sensibility, is not quite cricket. One could go on.

Teasing aside, this is not to claim an English monopoly on fair play, which would be palpably absurd. Some of the blackest chapters in sport, from Bodyline in the 1930s to the football hooliganism of the 1970s and 1980s, had their genesis in Britain. It is simply to highlight the small local variations – like local rules in golf – in perceptions of what is sporting and unsporting behaviour. Should one always be scrupulously honest? How single-mindedly should one pursue victory? When does tactical cunning become games-manship? And when does gamesmanship become cheating? You will get different answers in different countries.

But it would be foolish to get bogged down in semantics. Fair play is not a local eccentricity, peculiar to the British Isles, like warm beer or mushy peas, but part of the glue that binds the international sporting community together.

It was Shakespeare who first yoked the two words. They make their combined debut in the last act of *King John*, one of the most obscure plays in the canon, a rambling, unsatisfactory piece, the literary equivalent of Rotherham playing Macclesfield. The play is limping to its conclusion, when there they are suddenly, 'fair' and 'play', like a couple of gawky substitutes thrust into action in the eighty-second minute.

Philip Faulconbridge, an English lord, is raging against King John for striking a diplomatic deal with the papal legate, Pandulph:

> O inglorious league!
> Shall we, upon the footing of our land,
> Send fair-play orders and make compromise,
> Insinuation, parley and make truce
>   To arms invasive?

The tone is bitter, sarcastic. The exact meaning of the phrase 'fair-play orders' is murky, but Faulconbridge seems to be mocking the genteel courtesies of international diplomacy. It is an odd expression and, at a verbal level, does not quite come off. The substitution hasn't worked.

But Shakespeare does not give up. He tries the same combination of words again.

In the very next scene, the same character, Faulconbridge, has been sent as an emissary to the French Dauphin. He enters with his retinue and launches a formal address:

According to the fair play of the world,
Let me have audience . . .

And now, thrillingly, the substitution has worked. How snugly the two words fit together. It is as if they have never been apart. We must not bring anachronistic attitudes to the text. Shakespeare was not using 'fair play' in quite the sense a modern writer would – in Elizabethan usage, fairness had more to do with beauty than justice. Nor, when the Victorians evolved notions of fair play in sport, were they consciously quoting *King John*. But Shakespeare has coined the phrase and now, with a fine flourish, he has amplified it. 'The fair play of the world . . .' Casually, serendipitously, a great writer has put his finger on a great truth. It is not just a few random individuals who play fair. Fair play is universal. It is part of the unspoken compact that binds us together as human beings.

Again and again in sport – and perhaps that is why sport, at its best, stirs us so profoundly – we glimpse that grand Shakespearian universality. Mexicans and Swedes, Greeks and Ghanaians, Thais and Brazilians, Belgians and Costa Ricans: all united by the same quaint notions of how people should conduct themselves when they compete against each other in play. Sporting conventions have become a force for international good.

Let just one tiny example of that – the fair play of the world, transcending national differences – suffice for now.

In the international Venice Marathon in 1998, Daniele Caimmi of Italy and Wilfred Kibet of Kenya – two high-quality distance-runners, just short of the very top flight – were within 700 metres of the finish, neck and neck, when the Kenyan stumbled and fell. It was a rainy day and the course was slippery. Caimmi, gallantly, helped the other man to his feet. They resumed running, and the Kenyan narrowly won the race, with Caimmi back in second.

It was a low-profile event. Olympic glory was not at stake. But the gesture of goodwill – between two athletes who barely knew each other and did not speak the same language – was widely reported and admired.

The fair play of the world. In the city where Portia lectured Shylock on the quality of mercy, Daniele Caimmi had put flesh on Shakespeare's great phrase of four centuries before.

Fair play to him.

Jack Nicklaus: The Golden Bear

If fair play is intrinsic to good sportsmanship, it does not tell the whole story. The sportsman does not just compete fairly, in accordance with the rules. He knows that rules provide a basis for fair competition, but are not a guarantee of fair competition. He sees the bigger picture.

Nobody has ever exemplified that better than American golfer Jack Nicklaus, in one of the most celebrated of all sporting gestures.

The gimme – the short putt conceded to an opponent – is one of the glories of golf. There is nothing quite like it in any other sport. It plays no part in stroke-play tournaments, which account for the overwhelming majority of golf events seen on television. It is unique to match-play, in which players compete against each other, not the field.

At first glance, the gimme seems all of a piece with a game played by gentlemen. My dear sir, I won't insult you by asking you to hole that two-foot putt! Pick up your ball and we'll move on to the next hole! But the act of giving, as every golfer knows, is never pure. You give in the hope, nay expectation, of receiving the same courtesy in return. It's like Christmas. Auntie Gladys gives you a book token, you give Auntie Gladys a bottle of sherry. There is reciprocation, symmetry.

Watch a match-play event and you will hear the same expression again and again: 'Give give?' Golfer A, surveying a two-foot putt, looks hopefully at golfer B, surveying an eighteen-inch putt. B does the decent thing, and both players pick up their markers. Then at the next hole, the positions are reversed, and A does the decent thing. There is a lot of subtle by-play, leaving markers down 'for negotiating purposes' etc. A clever match-player will often concede a three-foot putt on one hole, then not concede a two-foot putt on the next hole. It is a game of cat and mouse running alongside the golf proper.

In my own case – and if there is a more timid, knock-kneed, wobbly-handed putter, I have yet to meet him – the perfect round of golf starts with my opponent left with a four-foot putt at the opening hole. I dart forward, pick up his ball and throw it to him. Too late, he realises he has been kippered. For the rest of the round, he either has to concede my four-foot putts or, if he makes me hole them, be left feeling like Ebenezer Scrooge.

But, of course, there is one situation, and one only, where the gimme cannot be reciprocated – on the eighteenth green, after the first player has holed out. To concede such a putt in a big match reveals generosity unsullied by self-interest – which is why the two-foot putt which Nicklaus conceded to Tony Jacklin at the end of the 1969 Ryder Cup has entered golfing folklore.

The Ryder Cup in the 1960s was a more low-key event than it is today. It was contested between the USA and Great Britain and Ireland, not between the USA and Europe, and was such a mismatch that an American victory could be taken for granted; all that was in doubt was the winning margin. When, in 1969, at Royal Birkdale, the underdog suddenly fought back, competing hard to the bitter end, it caught pundits by surprise.

The decisive match, fittingly, was contested by the leading player on each team: Jack Nicklaus for the United States and Tony Jacklin for Great Britain and Ireland. Nicklaus, the Golden Bear, was on his way to winning a record eighteen Majors. Jacklin, the golden boy of British golf, had just won his first Major, the 1969 Open at Lytham. It was a classic contest between the seasoned sheriff and the young gun-slinger and, after many twists and turns, it reached a classic denouement. When Jacklin was left with a two-foot putt on the last green – Nicklaus having holed a longer one – the result of the Ryder Cup depended on it. If he missed the putt, the Cup would go to America. If he holed it, the match would be tied.

Nicklaus knew, as every golfer knows, that the putt was missable. He had missed shorter putts himself, and seen his opponents do the same. The very next year, piquantly, at the 1970 Open at St Andrews, he would watch Doug Sanders miss a short putt on the final hole and hand him the title. But that was stroke-play, where conceded putts are inadmissible. This was match-play. And Nicklaus knew, not just the rules of match-play, but the spirit of match-play.

As he conceded Jacklin's putt – to the relief of the British player, who must have seen the possibility of disaster looming – he used words that bring a lump to the throat of every golf fan. 'I didn't think you were going to miss that one, but I didn't want to give you the opportunity.'

The opportunity, he might have added, to do something that will *haunt you all your life.*

Better not to win, Nicklaus reasoned, than to win at the expense of his opponent's humiliation. Better an honourable draw than victory with a sour aftertaste. And perhaps 'reasoned' is the wrong word. The Golden Bear didn't have time to reason things out: he just did the instinctive thing, the thing that came naturally. And because what came naturally was generous, altruistic, he showed himself, not just a great golfer, but a great man.

Elsewhere in the book, we will see sportsmen refusing to take advantage of the fact that an opponent was injured or an official had made a mistake. Their conscience was pricked by some unexpected happening and, because they had a well-developed sense of right and wrong, they did what their conscience told them. Nicklaus, for me, took chivalry to another level altogether. He realised that victory could also be rendered hollow if it caused a vanquished opponent too much hurt, crushing hurt, the kind of hurt that has no place in sport. He saw the bigger picture.

'I've often thought what I would have done in a similar position if the roles had been reversed,' Jacklin wrote in his autobiography. 'Of course it is only conjecture, but I like to think that I might have been as magnanimous as Nicklaus was on this occasion. I would like to think I would have been that big-hearted, but I don't know. We don't win the Ryder Cup all that often, so God knows what the captain would have said if I'd conceded a two-footer on the last!'

But Jacklin was clear about one thing: 'I would never have wanted to win that day because Nicklaus missed a putt. I've often been at golf matches and around greens and cringed when I heard fans whisper under their breath "Miss it" when someone they didn't want to win was standing over a putt. That makes me sick. There is no pride in winning that way. There is no satisfaction in winning because other people fall over.'

He was so touched by what Nicklaus had done that, later that evening, he sat down and wrote him a short letter of thanks. His respect for the American had risen exponentially. And he was not alone. Up to that point in his career, it is fair to say, Nicklaus had been more admired than loved. He was acknowledged as a formidable competitor, with an unrivalled record in the Majors. But he had never attracted the same kind of adulation as Arnold Palmer before him. There was a touch of the machine about him: the swing a tad mechanical, the haircut a tad severe. Now, suddenly, and in the most vivid way, he was showing his human side. Now, and for all time, he could be loved.

Look at the situation counter-factually for a moment. Nicklaus doesn't concede the putt. Jacklin misses it. Who loses? Jacklin, scarred for life by a traumatic, very public failure. (And scarred for life, incidentally, is no exaggeration. Ask Peter Alliss, who messed up the final hole in the 1953 Ryder Cup and has never forgotten it.) And who wins? Nobody! Yes, the Americans retain the Ryder Cup, but how many people will remember, forty years on, how they did it or even who played for them? They will only remember poor Tony Jacklin, fluffing a two-footer.

Now, still, and with gratitude, whether they are American or British, they remember the Golden Bear. Not a single golf shot he played – and he reeled them off with effortless brilliance for more than twenty years – has lodged in the memory as securely as this little moment of kindness, when he did not even have a golf club in his hand.

At the time, some of Nicklaus's Ryder Cup team-mates were furious with him: they thought he should have made Jacklin hole out. But the verdict of history is clear. That little gimme in the Ryder Cup has become so hallowed that there is now a championship golf course in Florida, co-designed by Nicklaus and Jacklin, called The Concession. A game played by gentlemen has achieved a fitting monument.

Could the same thing happen today, when the Ryder Cup enjoys a far higher profile and is far more intensely contested? It is hard to imagine so. The notion of winning ugly – grinding out results, not by outplaying the opposition, but by making fewer mistakes than them – has become a sporting mantra. Nobody thinks twice about humiliating an opponent; in fact, for many fans, the humiliation is all part of the fun. Witness the penalty shoot-out in football, a sadistic institution for a sadistic age: it throws the spotlight on the loser, not the winner. In golf, we don't want Tiger Woods to be spared having to hole a short putt. We want him to try to hole it and miss, so that we can relish his fallibility.

But even in a sadistic age, one thing is clear. If the next Ryder Cup does come down to a two-foot putt on the final green, glory will beckon – not for the player standing over the putt, but for his opponent. The voice of decency will whisper in his ear, very very faintly, like the breeze rustling the trees beside the green – and if he has got his wits about him, he will listen to it.

Jess Sweetser: A Gentleman in the Men's Room

Jack Nicklaus is such a regal figure, and the Ryder Cup such a high-profile event, that if you were to ask fifty golf fans what was the greatest act of sportsmanship in golf, all fifty of them would probably end up at the same spot, like golfers converging on the nineteenth hole after their round. Such is celebrity.

The legend of the Concession has grown and grown, with the great man not averse, on occasion, to pumping it up himself. But, inevitably, there are other candidates for the accolade of greatest act of golfing sportsmanship.

Who now remembers Jess Sweetser, the American who won the 1926 British Amateur Championship? He is just a name on a trophy, a trophy that has long since dwindled into insignificance. But he won the trophy with such a mixture of skill, physical courage, generosity and low cunning that you want to travel back in time and shake him by the hand.

Yale-educated Sweetser (second from the right in the photo opposite) was clearly an exceptional player. At the age of twenty he won the 1922 US Amateur Championship, giving Bobby Jones, no less, an 8-and-7 pasting in the semi-final, the heaviest defeat of his career. When he arrived at Muirfield in the summer of 1926 he was attempting to become the first American-born player to win the British amateur title.

Physically, he was feeling rotten, coughing continuously. He thought he just had a bad cold, or a case of 'flu, but was actually suffering from tuberculosis. It was not until the voyage home after Muirfield – when the ship's doctor placed him in quarantine – that the right diagnosis was made. The golfer would later spend long months in hospitals and sana-toriums.

But what was a hacking cough to a man on the threshold of sporting glory? Sweetser soldiered on and made it through to the final, where his opponent was A. F. Simpson, an Englishman. There was nothing wrong with Simpson's lungs. But there was something wrong with his car.

On the day of the final, it broke down outside North Berwick, causing Simpson to miss his tee time. The rules of the championship were clear and, although Simpson was des-perately trying to get to the course by other means, he would have to forfeit the match, an official explained to Sweetser.

The American was having none of it. He was not pre-pared to win the title by default, so he took evasive action, nipping into the clubhouse and locking himself in the lava-tory, where nobody could find him. 'I knew they would not let the title go unclaimed,' he said later. 'So I waited them out.'

An hour later, Simpson arrived on a bicycle, with his clubs strapped to his back. Battle was joined, and the man with the dodgy lungs beat the man with the dodgy car 6 and 5.

'It was a long way to travel to have something like a car determine the outcome of the match,' Sweetser later told friends back in America. He never made a great song and dance of the story. But how can one not admire the man at the heart of it, hiding in the lavatory to avoid being presented with the trophy he had sailed the Atlantic to win?

As with many of the older stories in the book, this one falls in the It Could Never Happen Today category. In 2009, Simpson would be driven to the course by a sponsored car and, if the tee time were delayed by as much as five minutes, the TV producer would be on the phone to the event organisers, demanding to know what the hell was going on. Sweetser would be tracked down, forced out of hiding and have a bank of microphones thrust in his face.

But the story also falls in the What a Shame It Could Never Happen Today category. That figure skulking in the lavatory, desperate for his opponent not to be disqualified, embodies the heroic lunacy of sport. The game must go on. It is the single greatest imperative in sport. And Jess Sweetser, insisting on playing, rather than winning by default, honoured the unspoken compact between sportsmen the world over.

In later life Sweetser became a stockbroker and, although he served on the editorial board of *The American Golfer*, was never quite an elder statesman in the Nicklaus league. But his human qualities were not forgotten.

On the day of his death, in 1989, the Georgia senator Sam Nunn paid touching tribute to him in Congress:

Each time I joined Jess for a game of golf and strolled down a fairway with him, I sensed that I was witnessing part of history . . . In golf, you often encounter players who have the ability to focus singly on the task at hand. Jess Sweetser was a man with a strong competitive drive, as evidenced by the record of his successes, but he was also a consummate gentleman. He would share his vast experience of the game as easily as one greets an old friend.

Perhaps golf is no more complicated than that. Or perhaps it is life that is not so complicated when it is enjoyed by a man of such grace and talent as Jess Sweetser. With Jess, life and golf were inseparable.

Perhaps we might wish he had found a more dignified hiding place in 1926. We cannot possibly wish he had behaved differently.

Ricky Ponting: Playing
for Laughs

Look in the lonely-hearts column of any English-language newspaper and you will see the same acronym with comic regularity. 'Male, 46, non-smoker, fit, but no oil painting, GSOH . . . female, Sagittarius, own car and cat, GSOH . . .' It is like the mating cry of birds, calling to each other across the vast prairie. Good looks are optional. A good sense of humour is essential.

It is certainly an essential ingredient in sportsmanship, that beautiful but elusive combination of qualities. Models of sporting behaviour must be honest. That goes without saying. They must act generously towards their opponents. That, too, goes without saying. They must possess a certain maturity of outlook, the ability to recognise situations where aggressive, competitive instincts need to be tempered. But also – not all the time, but some of the time – they have to know when to laugh. Professional sportsmen are not circus clowns: we would not treasure them if they were. But when laughter dies, sport dies. It is as simple as that.

The 2005 Ashes series furnished a memorable example of the role played by humour in sport. It featured the Australian captain Ricky Ponting who, by a nice irony, was guilty of a chronic sense-of-humour failure in the same series. When he was run out at Trent Bridge by a substitute fielder called Gary Pratt, the rest of us got the joke in seconds. But a furious Ponting could see nothing funny in his Pratt-fall, and departed in high dudgeon, effing and blinding his way back to the pavilion. To his credit, he later regained the moral high ground with some aplomb, giving Pratt two pairs of his boots, signed.

But it was at the final Test at the Oval that Ponting, his sense of humour restored, wrote his own little chapter in the annals of sportsmanship.

In a frustrating series for the Australian captain, Sunday 11 September was the most frustrating day yet. On paper, the Australians, who needed to win the match to level the series and retain the Ashes, were well placed to do just that. They started the day at 277-2 in their first innings, replying to 373 by England. The main obstacle was the weather: dark, low-lying clouds which, from early morning, settled over the Oval and stayed there. Ricky Ponting must have woken up in his hotel room, looked out of the window and felt physically sick. Weather delays had already taken time out of the match on the Friday and Saturday. Now it looked as if they were going to decide the entire fate of the Ashes.

There is nothing you can do about the weather. Every sportsman knows that. It is a fact of life. But it is a fact of life that some sportsmen accept more philosophically than others. The great Don Bradman once grumbled that expecting a batsman to bat on a rain-damaged pitch was like asking a billiard player to play on ripped baize. The Don was missing the point. The vagaries of the weather are part of the magnificent uncertainty of sport. Who will ever forget the climax to the 2008 Formula One season, Lewis Hamilton ploughing through rain puddles to clinch the fifth place he needed to win the championship? If the race had taken place in brilliant sunshine, it would have been a very dull affair.

But if bad weather cannot be helped, that does not make it any less cruel when you are on the receiving end. Ask Tim Henman, who would probably have won Wimbledon in 2001 if rain had not intervened at the worst possible time during his semi-final against Goran Ivanisevic. Ask Ricky Ponting, dealt an equally rotten hand at the Oval.

The Australians, forced to bat against Flintoff and Hoggard in atrocious light, collapsed to 367 all out, conceding a first-innings lead when they had hoped to gain one. Then, of course, as soon as England batted, the rules of the game changed completely. The umpires started fiddling with their light meters, the England batsmen scuttled back to the pavilion, and the Oval faithful – quite happy for it to rain for forty days and forty nights if it meant England regaining the Ashes – cheered their heads off. Cricket – the game of gentlemen, supposedly – can be the most brutal of all sports.

If ever a cricketer was entitled to shake his fist at the heavens, curse his fate, wallow in self-pity, it was Ponting, for whom those dark clouds, unless they dispersed soon, spelled disaster: the humiliation of being the first Australian captain in nearly twenty years to lose an Ashes series against the old enemy.

But self-pity has never been an Australian trait. It is certainly not a Ricky Ponting trait.

When the umpires finally judged light fit for play, and the Australian captain led his men out on to the field – in light that was playable, but only just – the entire Australian team was wearing sunglasses, as if playing in brilliant sunshine in Perth or Adelaide. It was a brilliant, puckish gesture: as charming as it was unexpected. *We can't do anything about your miserable Pommie weather, but we can see the funny side of it.* And twenty-five thousand Pommie fans got the joke and laughed in appreciation.

Mark Nicholas, commentating for Channel 4, was enchanted by the gesture. 'What a relief that people can still smile after all this drama!'

As play got under way, and the England batsmen had to face Shane Warne on a turning pitch, the tension was unbearable. Fans crouched on the edge of their seats. Nobody dared to miss a ball. But, after the comedy of the sunglasses, there was room for humour. People needed to laugh, if only to relieve the tension. Clouds loured overhead. The umpires consulted their light meters. There was a hint of drizzle in the air. In the stand by the gasometer, a group of England fans put up their umbrellas, trying to fool the umpires that it was raining. The Australian fans sitting in front of them promptly took off their shirts, as if expecting sunshine. Ripples of nervous laughter spread across the ground. It was only a game. It was only the most exciting, nerve-jangling cricket series ever played.

But it is one thing for spectators to play the clown, fool about, crack jokes. It is much rarer, much harder – it goes against the grain of everything the professional sportsman believes in – for players to do the same. Ricky Ponting leading out his men in sunglasses was a wonderful antidote to the dour scowls you see so often in other sports.

Ponting has had his detractors, like most high-profile sportsmen. But nobody can accuse him of not being able to laugh at himself. His little gesture at the Oval was like a coded love letter to the England fans. 'Tasmanian, mid-thirties, non-smoker, likes sport and beer, GSOH . . .'

Uncle Sam Discovers His Feminine Side

When I started researching this book I assumed that women would figure almost as prominently as men. The virtues that underpin sportsmanship – gentleness, consideration, sensitivity to the feelings of others – are quintessentially 'feminine' qualities, associated, in folklore, if not in science, with the female of the species. But, of course, for that very reason, they are unremarkable in a woman. We expect female athletes to behave well – they cannot ambush spectators with their sweetness, the way a male athlete can when he suddenly stops behaving like an-out-of-control child and melts into something softer.

To see Chris Evert on the tennis court was to see feminine sportsmanship in its purest form, elegance allied to good manners. But there was no sense of light and shade, no sense of a consuming passion for victory that would be tested by a poor line call, say. She was just too nice.

Some of the best stories of sportswomen acting chivalrously feature complete unknowns. Italian amateur skier
Gabriella D'Anzieri was just a bit-part player, the tiniest of
footnotes in sporting history. But her story contains humour
as well as honesty, mischief as well as magnanimity.

She was taking part in a minor slalom competition in
February 1988 and achieved the fastest time, beating men
and women alike. Unfortunately, because of a mistake by the
judges, who later admitted that they had not taken into
account the women's times, assuming that they would be
slower than the men's times, the trophy was awarded in error
to the fastest man.

There were red faces all round and, although there were
no cameras present, one can almost see those faces, twenty
years after the event: male chauvinism, Italian-style, all bluff
and bluster, caught with its trousers down. But D'Anzieri
refused to claim her rightful due.

'I do not want to be the cause of disappointment to a
young man who has already been proclaimed the winner,'
she said, with the insouciance of the true Corinthian. How
many men would have done the same?

And how many men would have shown the same good
sportsmanship as Mallory Holtman and Liz Wallace in a
college softball game in Ellensburg, Washington in April
2008?

I asked several American friends if they could remember
notable acts of sportsmanship, and this extraordinary
episode which, thanks to television, captured the imagination of fans across the States, featured on all their lists.
English sports fans may need a few footnotes (first clue:
softball is a modified form of baseball), but the basic human
story, revolving around a group of plucky, fresh-faced girls,
has universal appeal.

In fact, in many ways, the story is more English than American. The characters talk and behave as if they are from Dorking or Sevenoaks. It is like an episode from one of those Enid Blyton boarding-school stories of the 1950s, where Bunty has a pash on Betty, which upsets Milly, who sneaks to Georgy, who blubs to Hatty, and they all make it up over a bottle of pop at the dorm feast. There are tears, giggles and some absolutely spiffing heroines.

Western Oregon University were playing Central Washington University in the Great Northwest Athletic Conference, chasing an end-of-season play-off spot, when one of the Oregon team, diminutive twenty-one-year-old Sara Tucholsky, hit a home run, clearing the centre-field fence. It was the first time in her life she had hit a home run and, as this was her final year in college, was likely to be her last. She was so physically slight, and had such a modest record, that her suddenly slugging the ball out of the park would have been a good story in itself, like a No. 11 batsman hitting a six over the pavilion. Better still, as there were already players on two of the bases, it would have been a 'three-run homer'.

Normally with a home run the striker just jogs around the bases, lap-of-honour style, while the ball is retrieved. On this occasion, Tucholsky had only got as far as first base when she collapsed in agony on the ground, with torn ligaments in her knee. What to do? It was against the rules for her own team-mates to help her complete the home run, so one of the Washington players, Mallory Holtman, asked the umpire if it be OK if they helped her. A bemused umpire said there was nothing in the rules against it.

So Holtman and another Washington player, Liz Wallace, put their arms under Tucholsky's legs, and she put her arms over their shoulders. The three then headed around the bases, limbs splaying all over the place like a pantomime horse, stopping to let Tucholsky touch each base with her good leg.

'The only thing I remember is that Mallory asked me which leg was the one that hurt,' Tucholsky said afterwards. 'I told her it was my right leg and she said, "OK, we're going to drop you down gently and you need to touch it with your left leg", and I said, "OK, thank you very much."'

'She said, "You deserve it, you hit it over the fence", and we all just laughed.'

'We started laughing when we reached second base,' said Holtman. 'I said, "I wonder what this must look like to other people."'

'We didn't know this was her first home run,' said Wallace. 'That makes the story more touching than it was. We just wanted to help her.'

By the time the trio reached the home plate, the entire Western Oregon team was in tears. Inspired by Tucholsky's three-run homer, they went on to win the match 4-2, ending Central Washington's chances of winning the conference and advancing to the play-offs.

'In the end, it is not about winning and losing,' Holtman told reporters. 'She hit it over the fence, and was in pain, and she deserved a home run.'

As news of the episode spread, both Tucholsky and Holtman appeared on national television and radio, as well as receiving a stream of emails from sports fans. A YouTube video of the incident became required viewing, from New Hampshire to New Mexico. Chat-rooms sprang to life. Bloggers put in their two ha'p'orth. Thanks to the miracle of modern communications, a minor league game in a Cinderella sport, played on a remote pitch in front of fewer than a hundred spectators, had sent ripples across the nation.

'It's been magical and crazy at the same time,' said Tucholsky. 'I'm from a small town, and actually pretty shy, so all this is strange to me. I'm surprised at how many people have paid attention to this and how far the story has gone. But there are so many negative images of athletes now. Here's a positive image.'

'I just thought it was something anyone would have done,' said Holtman modestly. 'It's really cool that people have responded to this so positively.'

It was not all bouquets and roses. One blogger labelled Holtman a selfish player who did not consider her team-mates. Tucholsky received an email criticising women's lack of competitive spirit. There was much debate about whether the same thing could, or should, have happened in an all-male sport.

'Some people are trying to say this is something men would never have done,' said the Western Oregon coach Pam Knox. 'I think that's an unfair statement. You would hope guys would have the character to do the right thing at the right time.' Others disagreed.

But, one way or another, the blue touchpaper had been lit. A single moment of generosity, in a world unaccustomed to it, had achieved a searing impact, jogging consciences, inflaming imaginations.

A few months later, at the ESPY awards in Los Angeles – the sports equivalent of the Oscars – the three women received the award for Best Sports Moment, sharing the limelight with the likes of Tiger Woods, Roger Federer and David Beckham. The award was voted for by the public, which was also significant. It was not just a few soppy women who loved what they had seen in Ellensburg. The episode also tickled the kind of hard-core male fans who hang out in sports bars, have stomachs the size of the Grand

Canyon and whoop 'Get in the hole!' at golf tournaments. It was as if a whole sporting culture had suddenly paused, taken stock and re-evaluated its priorities.

In America, even more than in Europe, winning is paramount. You don't play sport to take part, you play to beat the other guys and show you are top dog. The sporting lexicon is dominated by Rambo-like metaphors. Players in every sport, from golf to ice hockey, are urged to step up to the plate, walk tall, hang tough. Most of all, they are expected to kick ass or, better still, whup ass. 'It's all bottoms with you Americans, isn't it?' complained Basil Fawlty. The plucky loser, an iconic figure in Britain, is just a wimp Stateside. Here, suddenly, was a different narrative, shot through with tenderness: players from opposing teams not just respecting each other, but prepared, in certain situations, to help each other. Cooperation, not confrontation. Giving, not taking. Smiles, not snarls. An entire new way of interacting on the sports field.

'The two teams are wrapped in a bond of good feeling we can only wish did not seem so singular, so remarkable,' wrote veteran sports columnist George Vecsey in the *New York Times*. If the same thing had happened in a baseball World Series, and a player had collapsed to the ground, the attitude of the opposing coach would have been: 'Let him lie there.' The stakes would have been too high.

But, even at the highest level, Vecsey reflected, examples of good sportsmanship are not unknown. 'Maybe sportsmanship is universal, out there, needing to be cultivated.'

Exactly.

Jimmy Connors Serves
a Double

If the college softball story highlights the need for sport to get in touch with its feminine side, it also illustrates something else – the importance of knowing when to apply rules flexibly.

Not all umpires are idiots, and not all the legislators who draft the rules are idiots, but there are times, in every sport, when the two combine to create totally farcical situations. In Ellensburg, it was crazy enough that an injured player should have to complete the formalities of a home run, when the ball had been hit out of the park: it was even more crazy that the injured player could be helped by the other team, but not her own team. The rules, in short, were not equal to an unforeseen situation. It was only quick thinking by the Central Washington players, rather than the umpires exercising discretion, that saved the day. They found an ingenious, even witty, way of ensuring that justice was done.

Jimmy Connors showed equal quick-wittedness in the final of the 1975 Australian Open in Melbourne. At issue was that bane of professional tennis players before and since – the dodgy line call.

Now that Hawkeye and the appeal system have lessened the impact of poor line calls, tennis has entered a less fractious age, and not before time. It *was* frustrating, in a big match, when a vital point was awarded to the wrong player because some decrepit line judge, dressed like a P. G. Wodehouse character, took his/her eye off the ball. But those moments of incompetence by officials did provide fascinating insights into the characters of the players. Would the player who had been robbed of the point throw a wobbly, lose concentration? Or would he shrug off the disappointment and come back stronger than before? And how about the other player, the beneficiary of the mistake? Would he cash in ruthlessly or do the decent thing?

There have been plenty of well-documented instances of top players refusing to take advantage of a mistake by an official. In the 2005 ATP Masters in Rome, Andy Roddick was on match point in his second-round match when his opponent, Fernando Verdasco, served what was, wrongly, called a double fault. Roddick pointed out the mistake and went on to lose the match. But the Jimmy Connors episode, in its way, is even more noteworthy: first, because it was a Grand Slam final; secondly, because of the personality of the player involved.

Connors, bristling with aggression on and off the court, was not most people's idea of a model sportsman. When he swept Ken Rosewall aside in the 1974 Wimbledon final, it was like a changing of the guard in tennis. Out went the old traditions, the old courtesies; in came something rawer, brasher, less gracious. Suddenly it was not just all right to grunt on the tennis court, it was all right to challenge and browbeat officials. The Age of John McEnroe – expletive-laced tantrums, at once demeaning and hugely entertaining – was just a few years away.

A law graduate of UCLA, Illinois-born Connors had earned a reputation as a maverick as well as an explosive tennis player. In 1972 he refused to join the newly formed Association of Tennis Professionals (ATP), signing a contract with the rival World Team Tennis (WTT). When not on the tennis court, he always seemed to be plotting or filing law-suits. He was one of those awkward, combative, contrary types who can start an argument in an empty room.

By the time of the 1975 Australian Open, played on the grass courts of Kooyong, Connors was at the zenith of his career. He had won three Grand Slam titles the previous year and was in the middle of an extraordinary 160-week run as world no. 1, a record only overtaken by Roger Federer in 2007. His opponent in the final was the hard-bitten Australian John Newcombe, a great champion in his own right, but now well past his peak. He had had a much tougher passage to the final than Connors, so the American was the red-hot favourite. But things did not go according to script – they seldom do in sport.

Newcombe took the first set, Connors the second. It was a hard-fought match, but the momentum was with the younger man. The critical moment came in the third set. Connors, serving at 2-3, was 40-15 up, courtesy of two out-rageous line calls, one of them an 'ace' that was well out. The Australian crowd made their feelings known – at which point Connors, ostentatiously, puckishly, served a double fault.

It was a moment of pure sporting whimsy, so unexpected that nobody knew quite how to react. Newcombe later said he thought it was one of the silliest things he had ever seen. But the immediate objective – to win back the crowd, show that he was a nice guy underneath, the sort that fair-dinkum Aussie fans would appreciate – had been achieved. It was only a light-hearted gesture, as Connors saw it, not a deliberate pushing of the self-destruct button.

A gesture, moreover, in the finest traditions of sport. Yes, it was clumsy, improvised, slightly coarse in conception. If Connors felt guilty about the 'ace' he had been donated by the line judge, surely the sensible thing would have been to insist that *that* point was replayed? But one has to give Connors marks for ingenuity. Officialdom had thwarted the crowd's hunger for a fair fight with a fair outcome. Officialdom had to be put in its place. In terms of sportsmanship, it was not just a generous, but elegant, gesture, the more elegant for being so unexpected.

But the momentum of the match had subtly shifted: it was as if, in the battle of wills, Connors had blinked first, showing a lack of ruthlessness which, to a sporting opponent, is always going to look like weakness. The double fault took the score to 40-30, giving Newcombe an opening which, with all the ruthlessness Connors had lacked, he exploited. The underdog bit back, levelling to deuce, taking the set 6-4, then going on to win the fourth set as well. It was the last and, in many ways, most improbable of his Grand Slam titles.

Newcombe took the match 7-5, 3-6, 6-4, 7-5. How little figures in a record book capture the real drama of the occasion. An intense, bruising encounter, between two great champions, illuminated by this sudden outpouring of generosity, comically out of kilter with what had gone before. *I owe you a point, John Newcombe. Here it is, for free, gift-wrapped!* Then back to the business of competition.

Nothing in Connors' later playing career became him as well as this little moment of sportsmanship in Melbourne. He quickly reverted to type: brash, aggressive, argumentative, an emotional powder keg, liable to explode at any minute. In 1986, with his talents on the wane, he was fined $20,000 and suspended for ten weeks after a spat with officials in a tournament in Florida. He often gave the impression of a man trying to out-McEnroe McEnroe. An angry man, a driven man, a competitor so ferocious that it was only when he stopped competing, and retired from tennis, that we could begin to love him.

Today, the myth of Jimmy Connors the Brat is so entrenched that, if you were to ask a sports fan which great tennis player once deliberately double-faulted in a Grand Slam final, they would never guess the answer unless they knew it already. They would assume it was one of the good guys, the gentlemen of the game – Stan Smith, Ken Rosewall, Stefan Edberg.

But it was Jimmy Connors, and we should not forget that it was. Like many a sportsman before and since, he deserves a more complex epitaph than he is likely to get. Look at it this way. How many tennis players can claim to have served a great double fault?

Connors certainly chose the perfect setting for his sportsmanship. Australians are not just passionate about sport, but passionate about the spirit of sport. They have their Achilles heel – sledging – but they also have an almost romantic attachment to the notion of chivalrous competition.

Referees in the Premier League get such a non-stop diet of abuse from managers and players that there is an air of inevitability about the whole process. It would be nice if it did not happen, but so many people would have to change their attitudes so radically for it not to happen, that, for football fans, the abuse has become a fact of life.

It is worth contrasting that situation with the Australian experience and, in particular, with the weird and wonderful Brownlow Medal, which is presented annually to the outstanding player in the Australian Football League – the equivalent of the PFA Player of the Year award. To someone brought up on soccer or rugby, AFL rules, which blend elements from both codes, take a bit of getting used to. But you do not have to understand the rules to grasp the significance of the Brownlow Medal, which was first awarded in 1924 and named after a famous Geelong player, Charles Brownlow.

The medal goes to 'the fairest and best player', which is a good story in itself, evidence of a sport with its heart in the right place. But the true glory of the Brownlow – truly mind-blowing if you are an English soccer fan – is who chooses the winner of the medal at the end of the season. Not the players. Not the managers. Not the fans. Not the sportswriters. The *umpires.*

Try imagining the same thing happening in the Premier League. It is quite impossible. Referees are lucky if they leave the field without abuse ringing in their ears. The idea of trusting them to arbitrate something as prestigious as a Player of the Year award belongs to science fiction. It is like a reversion to childhood, with the games master doubling as referee or umpire, then writing the end-of-term report cards. He is a figure of authority, a guardian of sporting standards.

With the Brownlow, the three on-field officials award points to players after each match and cast their votes in the strictest secrecy. Elaborate steps are taken to avoid any suggestion of impropriety. Armoured security vehicles have sometimes been used to transport the ballot boxes to the venue where the award is announced. It is a complicated, bureaucratic system, but its merits are obvious – the chief one being that players with a poor disciplinary record are effectively out of the running. You will not win the Brownlow if you bad-mouth the officials. Good manners have been placed at the symbolic heart of the sport.

Australian officials are as fallible as officials the world over – hence the need for Jimmy Connors to serve a double fault in 1975. But a great sporting nation does not lightly throw its erring officials to the wolves. It honours them for their experience and know-how.

Robbie Fowler and
That Penalty*

If some sporting gestures are glorious, uplifting, whole-hearted, others are incomplete, unsatisfying – which explains the asterisk in the title of this chapter. I am not convinced that footballer Robbie Fowler belongs in the same pantheon as Flintoff, Nicklaus and the other gods of sportsmanship.

If I were to assert that Ghanaians, say, had higher moral standards than Estonians, I would be condemned on all sides. Even if I stood my ground, and explained that I had spent two blissfully happy years in Ghana but, on my only visit to Estonia, been mugged, robbed and served by the rudest waitress I have encountered east of Paris, my views would carry no weight whatsoever. They would be seen not only as racist but as intellectually untenable.

But suppose I were to advance the same argument in

relation to golfers and footballers? Would it be quite so ridiculous? Quite so indefensible?

The fact is that, in my years as a sporting couch potato, I must have watched thousands of hours of televised football and almost as much televised golf. And, as anyone who has done the same will corroborate, it has been like watching two different ethical universes.

Do golfers feign injury, abuse officials, head-butt their opponents, make V-signs at the crowd, claim that they have been elbowed in the face when they have had a slight knock on the little toe? Of course not. They have an unwritten code of good conduct to which, with very few exceptions, they stick. It is football, the world game, which has dragged the good name of sport into the gutter.

Quite why that should be, and how standards of behaviour in football can be improved, is the subject for another book. But it has certainly hampered my search for iconic moments of sportsmanship.

I have a friend, an Arsenal fan, whom I will call P to spare his blushes. I consulted him, as I consulted many of my friends. Could he remember any Arsenal matches notable for sporting conduct? Had Arsène Wenger ever sent flowers to a referee he had insulted? Had Martin Keown or Jens Lehmann ever said 'We were beaten by the better team on the day?'

P looked stunned. The question had taken him into uncharted waters. He thought and thought. Nothing came. Then he suddenly slapped his thigh. 'Of course! Robbie Fowler!'

'You mean—'

'That penalty!'

'Of course!'

At which we both abased our heads, and like cricket fans

remembering Bob Willis bowling down the hill at Headingley in 1981, became all maudlin and misty-eyed.

It must have been an Arsenal–Liverpool match at Highbury in the mid-nineties – 1996, I later discovered. Robbie Fowler, for Liverpool, ran into the penalty area, stumbled and fell. The referee whistled and pointed to the spot. And Fowler, incredibly, got to his feet and gestured that it had not been a penalty – he had just tripped.

'I remember it as if it was yesterday,' said P. 'Extraordinary.'

'Extraordinary,' I agreed. 'But hang on. If it's the match I'm thinking of, didn't Fowler then take the penalty anyway? The goalie saved it, but some other Liverpool player scored from the rebound.'

'Did he? Oh dear. That spoils it, doesn't it?'

'It does rather.'

Better half a loaf than no bread, of course. In an age when footballers routinely claim penalties when they have not even been touched by an opponent, Fowler's little moment of honesty shines like a good deed in a naughty world. But no sporting romantic will ever feel satisfied by the episode. If Fowler knew it wasn't a penalty, why cynically profit from the referee's blunder? Why not do the Corinthian thing and, instead of taking the penalty, kick the ball out of play or pass it back to the goalkeeper? Good sportsmanship is absolute. You're either sporting or you're unsporting. You can't be half-sporting. The very idea is a nonsense.

'He probably just did what he thought his manager would want him to do,' said P mournfully.

Well, there is that, of course.

There is an interesting postscript to the Fowler story, which bears out my theory about ethics, or the lack of them, in professional football. Every sphere of human activity has its idealists, people who strive for purity and dream of an international order based on honesty and decency. In sport, as well as the International Olympic Committee, there is the International Committee for Fair Play, an obscure coalition of the great and the good, now based in Hungary, which works to promote the ideals of sportsmanship.

I have no quarrel with the work of the ICFP. Their values are unimpeachable – although their implementation of them, swilling with international good intentions, and wrapped up in Euro-speak, has a comically Clouseau-esque quality. Here, for example, is the citation for Richard Blakey, one of only two cricketers ever to be honoured by the ICFP:

> During a game on 14 July 1994, he stopped a ball thrown by the opponent Whitaker (who had already scored 35 points) with a reflex movement. Everybody considered his catch a very good one, but Blakey spontaneously said he had caught the ball after it had just touched the ground. This allowed his opponent batsman to obtain 139 points.

I *think* I can work out what happened, but it's not Neville Cardus, is it?

The only other cricketer to have caught the eye of the ICFP is Cecil Browne of Fiji:

> During a competition against Kenya in the quarter-finals of an international tournament, a batsman from the opposite team continued running although the ball had been stopped. According to regulations, the player should be eliminated. However, Browne, the captain of the Fiji team, told the player from Kenya to go back to his position.

With this one, I am at a total loss. What actually happened? I am sure I could find out if I consulted *Wisden*. I prefer to let the citation stand as a monument to the irreducible English-ness of cricket. The game has never been understood on the Continent, and never will be.

Having missed the point of cricket, the ICFP also seems to have missed the point of the Fowler incident. Its 1996 awards list includes a diploma for 'Robert B. Fowler of Liverpool' for signalling to the referee that he had not been fouled in the Arsenal penalty area. The obvious snag – if Robert B. Fowler knew he had not been fouled, why did he take the penalty? – seems to have been brushed under the carpet. Presumably, and one can sympathise, the ICFP had trouble finding any footballer, in any country, who had done anything gallant or praiseworthy that year.

It all seems so unfair. The football millionaire, for a half-hearted, half-cock gesture, gets a diploma for good behaviour to pin to his living-room wall, while the journeymen of sport – the honest-to-God runners and swimmers and hockey players – go unrewarded. It is as if, in wartime, soldiers in the Green Jackets and Parachute Regiment had to charge an enemy machine-gun position single-handed to earn a VC, while soldiers in the Liverpool Light Infantry only had to turn up on parade on time with clean boots and a parting in their hair.

Or am I being unfair to the ICFP? The more I ponder the Fowler penalty incident, the more something strikes me.

That friend of mine, P, the Arsenal fan with difficulty getting his head around the notion of sportsmanship. A decade on from the Liverpool match, he had totally forgotten that Fowler had gone on to take the non-penalty. He had totally forgotten the score in the match. But he had retained, as I had, an indelible physical image: a Premier League footballer, in the opposition penalty area, frantically gesturing to the referee that he had not been fouled. It was a jaw-dropping piece of television: one of those 'Did I really see that or have I switched to the History Channel by mistake?' moments.

How can one measure the potency of such televised images in the popular imagination? It was a split-second gesture, the equivalent of a line of dialogue in a three-hour play. Yet it had an unexpectedness, an integrity, that resonated far beyond its immediate context. Robbie Fowler is no saint. His infamous taunting of Graeme le Saux was inexcusable. But in the iconography of modern football, because of the Arsenal penalty incident, he will forever be identified with the Honest Centre Forward – a mythical figure, to be sure, but a mythical figure whom the game has never needed more. What is football, what is any sport, without its myths of heroic behaviour?

In fairness to other sportsmen featured in the book – who would have deigned to take a penalty they had not earned – the asterisk against Fowler's name must stand. But, if only as someone who briefly rose above the cynicism of his sport, he belongs in their company.

Judy Guinness: Too Honest
for Her Own Good

Erratic officiating is the bane of many sports. When it is a man on the receiving end, you fear the worst: clenched fists; four-letter words; a Vesuvian eruption of indignation. When it is a woman, the outlook is generally – though not invariably – rosier.

It is hard not to be touched by the tale of Heather 'Judy' Guinness, who fenced for Great Britain at the 1932 Olympics in Los Angeles (on the left in the photo above). She is a shadowy figure, long dead, but somehow, simply from her actions, you feel you know her. She had an aristocratic, Anglo-Irish pedigree. Her father, Henry Seymour Guinness, travelled in the Far East, then became a Senator of the Irish Free State. But in her quiet integrity there is something indelibly British. Walk into a tearoom in Harrogate or a library in Melton Mowbray and you will see a Judy Guinness sitting there: sober, sensibly dressed, a pillar of her community; fresh-faced; no make-up; jolly of manner, but with a hint of steel; phlegmatic in adversity.

Her fifteen minutes of sporting fame occurred at a time when the very idea of women breaking into a sweat to try to win something was still vaguely revolutionary. In that sense, Judy Guinness was ahead of her times. To her true British phlegm, one must add a soupçon of romantic dash. Only a woman born to adventure would have travelled halfway around the world, at the age of twenty-one, to fence for her country.

The Los Angeles Olympics, held during the Depression, reflected the greyness of the times. There were fewer competitors than there had been in Amsterdam four years earlier: it was just too far to travel. Proceedings had an amateurish air. The women's 100m final was won by an athlete from Poland who, it later emerged, had both male and female genitalia. In the hockey, the host team won the bronze medal in the most farcical circumstances: only three teams entered and, as the USA were thrashed 24-1 by India, one surmises that they were an embarrassment, stepping sheepishly on to the podium.

One of the few specks of colour was provided by the women. In the first modern Olympics in 1896, there were no female competitors at all. Baron Pierre de Coubertin, the founding father of the Olympic movement, had no place for women in his grand sporting vision. But history was on the march. Women may only have accounted for about 10 per cent of the competitors in Los Angeles, but their impact was far greater than that. They stayed in a luxury hotel, the Chapman Park, and were feted wherever they went. There were so few of them – Judy Guinness was one of only 126 female competitors – that they had the glamour of pioneers.

And, like pioneers, they had to hack it over rough terrain. The officiating at the Games, despite technological innovations like automatic timers and photo-finish cameras, was execrable. Cock-up followed cock-up. Controversy spawned controversy. In the men's steeplechase, the runners were inadvertently made to run an extra lap. In the 5000m, there was uproar when, after deliberating for two hours, the judges awarded the gold medal to a Finn, Lauri Lehtinen, who had impeded the American hopeful, Ralph Hill. The result of the 100m final – officially won by Eddie Tolan by one inch from Ralph Metcalfe – is disputed to this day.

Amid such an orgy of blunders, winning and losing became a lottery. Time muddies the waters. We can feel reasonably certain that the Indians did beat the Americans at hockey: that 24-1 score line has the ring of truth. But with some of the other events, who knows? Perhaps the judges got it wrong. One American reporter joked that it might be a good idea if the photographers taking snaps of the winners told the judges who had won – that way, they could know without waiting to read the newspapers the next day.

Human nature being what it is, when the officials have a bad day it rubs off on the competitors, who lose confidence in the whole process. They cannot rely on a fair outcome to the contest, so they box clever, put their faith in luck. They develop a feral streak: if they get a lucky break, however undeserved, they squirrel it away against the time when they get an unlucky break.

Unless they happen to be Judy Guinness.

The judging in the fencing hall was as eccentric as on the track. Guinness, competing in the individual foil, made it through to the final, where she took on Austrian Ellen Preis. It was a close-fought contest, with nothing to separate the two women. At one point, the judges missed a hit on

Guinness by Preis. Then they missed another one. It was going to be her day. When the points were totted up, she had won by just one point, becoming, hallelujah, the first *ever* British fencer to take Olympic gold.

You can guess the rest. O Judy, Judy. Even after all these years, you know what she is going to do, and why she is going to it. You can see her upper lip stiffen as she goes over to the judges, tells them about the two hits they have missed, concedes gold to her opponent, has to settle for silver. She's twenty-one. She's just a girl. She doesn't know any better. And you love her for not knowing better, for not having developed the cynicism that says: 'So I got lucky. Big deal. The officials messed up. Rub of the green. Whatever.'

How very naive. How very honourable.

Jean Shiley: Making the Cut

If Judy Guinness took the honours for good sportsmanship at Los Angeles, she was run mighty close by American Jean Shiley, who took the gold medal in the high jump, after another bizarre piece of officiating.

Shiley was born in 1912 in Harrisburg, Pennsylvania, sister of three younger brothers. She was a country girl, a tomboy. Even after her athletic abilities had been recognised, and she received proper high-jump coaching, there was something gloriously amateurish about her training. She practised in her back yard by jumping over a fishing rod balanced between two clothes-line supports. Her traditionally minded father, a car mechanic, hated his daughter having anything to do with athletics. He never once saw her compete.

But compete Shiley did and, despite much tut-tutting from her family, sailed to Europe to take part in the 1928

Amsterdam Olympics, finishing a tantalising fourth in the high jump. She was still only sixteen, and a star in the making – although she had to share the sporting firmament with an even brighter star, Mildred 'Babe' Didrikson.

Didrikson, an iconic American figure and one of the most gifted all-round athletes ever, got her nickname from Babe Ruth after hitting five home runs in a single baseball match when she was still a girl. In later life, as Babe Zaharias, she was the outstanding woman golfer of her generation. There seemed to be almost nothing at which she did not excel. She sang hit singles. She was a brilliant basketball player. In 1931, she won the Texas sewing – yes, sewing – championship. You name it, the Babe did it – and did it consummately. She could probably have arm-wrestled Johnny Weissmuller.

Modesty, it has to be said, was not her strong suit. Didrikson was famously cocky and far more popular among fans than she was with her fellow athletes. One needs to remember that to grasp the magnitude of the generosity which Jean Shiley showed her.

Patronisingly framed rules decreed that women could only compete in three events, or heaven knows how many medals Didrikson might have won at Los Angeles. As it was, she had to settle for the javelin, the 80m hurdles and the high jump. She took the javelin comfortably, but was then involved in a virtual dead heat with Evelyne Hall in the hurdles.

A photograph shows the two women neck and neck at the tape. Didrikson then threw up her arm in an effort to sway the judges – an old trick. The judges dithered, reviewed inconclusive photos and eventually declared Didrikson the winner, recording the same time – 11.7 seconds, a new world record – for both women.

Hall never came to terms with the verdict. As late as 1990 – Olympic dreams never die, they just grow old – she gave an interview claiming that she should have had a share of gold. Like everyone else, she resented Didrikson's arrogance, her condescension to her rivals. When the Babe was interviewed in the *Los Angeles Times* after the race, she exuded cockiness. 'Sure, I slowed up a little . . . I just wanted to make it a good race. Win the next event? Well, I hope so. That's what I'm here for.' It was on to the high jump.

If the fans were eager to see if this new American superstar could make it a hat-trick, the mood among her fellow competitors was very, very different. Several of them sought out Jean Shiley in her room at the Chapman Park hotel. The message was unanimous: 'We couldn't beat her, Jean. You've just *got* to beat her, cut her down to size.'

Were the Fates listening? Did they want to punish Didrikson for her hubris? They certainly did their best to level things out. The high jump, like the hurdles, was too close to call. Shiley and Didrikson both cleared 5 foot 5 inches – a world record – and both failed at 5 foot 6 inches. The bar was reset at 5 foot 5½ inches for a jump-off. Both women cleared the bar, at which point the judges made their decisive, controversial intervention.

As a high-jumper, as in so much else, Didrikson was a trailblazer. She used a technique known as the Western Roll, a precursor of the Fosbury Flop, leading with her head and upper body. Nothing wrong in that, you might think, but the rules then in force specifically outlawed 'diving', and the method was controversial. On this occasion the judges ruled that her head had crossed the bar before her feet, and that the jump was therefore a foul. Gold to Shiley, silver to Didrikson, and a loud raspberry for the judges. For heaven's sake! If they objected to the

Western Roll, why didn't they warn Didrikson earlier in the competition? Or why not let her retake the jump? Why bring the whole event to a shuddering anti-climax with their pernicketiness?

At this remove of time one feels only qualified sympathy for Didrikson. Yes, she had been 'robbed' of a hat-trick of gold medals by over-zealous officiating. But she also comes across as an arrogant, graceless competitor, the sort one does-n't mind seeing brought down a peg or two.

But there is no need to qualify one's admiration for Shiley. She had done what her friends had asked her: she had cut Babe Didrikson down to size. But she still managed to be magnanimous in victory – and to express that magnanimity in the most ingenious way.

At the end of the games, in a marvellous gesture, she offered to have the two medals cut in half, and the gold and silver halves joined together, for each athlete to take home. Just symbolism, of course, but symbolism at its potent best, in the highest Olympic tradition. The action of a true sportswoman.

And her reward? It makes you angry even to think about it. Shiley, naturally, like any successful Olympian, was eager to compete in the next games, in Berlin in 1936. In the summer of 1933 she graduated from Temple University in Pennsylvania and, strapped for cash, worked briefly as a swimming teacher, and was paid for her services – a breach of the amateur code.

Officialdom, in the person of Dan Ferris of the US Olympic Committee, reacted with brutal intransigence. Shiley was barred from the American team, on grounds of professionalism, despite her desperate appeals. She never got the chance to defend her title in Berlin, and had to find work as a typing instructor. In later life, she married a physicist and had three children.

After the war, when Babe Didrikson – now Babe Didrikson Zaharias, star of the LPGA golf tour – was playing a tournament in her area, the two rivals from Los Angeles would meet up for a reunion and talk about the good old days. A whole world of disappointment and regret can sometimes seem to separate gold and silver. Here, beautifully, the two had become one.

Vera Caslavska: Dignity under Duress

Another Olympics, more dreadful judging and another woman bearing herself impeccably amidst the mayhem. This time there was a new ingredient in the cocktail – politics.

Czech gymnast Vera Caslavska – a diminutive blonde with a frolicsome mop of hair – could hardly have competed in the 1968 Olympics in Mexico City in less auspicious circumstances. At Tokyo four years earlier she had dominated her discipline, winning three gold medals. But two months before the Mexico City games, Russian tanks rolled into Czechoslovakia. Caslavska, a prominent figure in the Prague Spring, the pro-democracy movement snuffed out by the Soviets, was warned that she was in danger of being arrested and fled to the mountains, where she had to continue her training in ludicrous circumstances, doing floor exercises in meadows, swinging from the branches of trees, even lifting sacks of potatoes to keep up her body strength. She was only given permission to compete at the Games at the last minute.

Gymnastics judging is a murky business at the best of times, riddled with political bias, but in an event where her main rivals were gymnasts from the Soviet Union and judges from the Soviet Bloc dominated the panel, Caslavska was on a hiding to nothing. She was widely expected to win gold on the beam, as she had in Tokyo, but was controversially consigned to second place by her Soviet rival, Natalia Kuchinskaya. A few neutral eyebrows – no, more than a few – were raised at the scores.

The floor exercises saw the same depressing pattern repeat itself. Caslavska, with a witty improvisation on a Mexican hat dance, appeared to have won gold outright when, in a last-minute piece of tinkering, the judges decided to upgrade the preliminary scores of Larissa Petrik, another Soviet gymnast. The gold was shared – which meant that Caslavska had to step on to the podium with a competitor from the country which had just invaded her homeland.

Her understated protest – she did share the podium with the Russian but, when the Soviet national anthem was played, turned her head pointedly away – won her widespread admiration and sympathy. At the end of the competition, when she married a fellow Czech athlete, ten thousand Mexicans surrounded the church to wish the couple well.

At this remove of time, the restraint which Caslavska showed – making her point, but in a dignified way, without flouting the spirit of Olympic competition – seems wholly admirable, in the highest sporting traditions. One could argue all day and all night about the rights and wrongs of mixing politics and sport. An Olympic purist might argue that any political gesture on the podium was inappropriate. Others would go the other way and wish the Czech gymnast had been far more outspoken. For me, what is touching, and indicative of good sportsmanship, is her respect for her Russian opponent. Her quarrel was not with her: it was with Leonid Brezhnev, the Soviet leader.

Caslavska could have gone the whole hog – as Tommie Smith and John Carlos did with their famous Black Power salutes at the same Olympics – but preferred a more muted, ladylike form of protest.

Needless to say, it was not muted enough for the Czech authorities. For the best part of twenty years, Caslavska was *persona non grata* in her own country, denied the right to travel abroad, publish her autobiography or even take part in sports events. It was a demoralising, frustrating period, and only her natural feistiness pulled her through. All her gymnastic agility was powerless against the inflexibility of the Communist placemen in Prague.

On 3 January 1970 she asked the sports minister for a job with the national girls' gymnastics team. He refused, saying: 'Come back next year. This is not a suitable time yet.' For five years, every 3 January, she appeared in the same office, asking for the same job, with the same result. Deadlock.

'For the fifth year,' she recalled later, in an interview for the *New York Times*, 'I was supposed to apply again, but I knew it was necessary to change my way of negotiations. So I dressed in an aerobics suit, high at the neck, very tight. I am quite a conservative person, and it was hard for me to dress like that, but I had to look for my courage. The sports minister looked at me and measured me with his eyes. He asked me: "Vera, what have you got on? Are you crazy?" I answered him: "No, but I was supposed to come back on 3 January, and apply for work, and now I'm here, dressed for work. And I'm not leaving until you give me a team and a gymnastics hall in which to work.'"

It was a bold, full-frontal sally, and it achieved its objective. Caslavska *was* given coaching work but, because of her opposition to Communism, only under conditions of extreme secrecy. In 1979, after the Mexican government reputedly threatened to cease oil exports to Czechoslovakia, she was given permission to work as a coach in Mexico. But in her own country she remained an outcast.

It was only with the overthrow of Communism in 1989 that she was finally rehabilitated. She served as chairwoman of the Czech Olympic Committee, and as personal adviser to Vaclav Havel, the new President. There was talk of her becoming ambassador to Japan. But her emergence into the sunlight was short-lived, overshadowed by a tragedy in her private life. She had divorced her husband in 1987 but, six years later, her son was imprisoned for stabbing his father to death at a disco – an episode which plunged the great gymnast into deep depression. For ten years, she became a virtual recluse.

How little of the thrilling exuberance she had displayed in the gymnastics hall endured! 'My medals just remind me of my youth,' she said wistfully, as she approached her sixtieth birthday. 'Human values are more important.'

But beneath the wistfulness she was right. Human values are more important. Forty years on, the quiet courage which she displayed on the podium at Mexico City still brings a lump to the throat. It was as dextrous a gesture as the most athletic of somersaults.

John Landy: Senseless Chivalry

In 2002, when a statue entitled 'Sportsmanship' was unveiled opposite Olympic Park in Melbourne, there were few arguments about the athlete represented by the statue. If Sir Don Bradman was Australia's greatest ever sportsman, Sir John Landy, later Governor of Victoria, was the one forever associated with chivalry and good sporting manners: a true national icon.

Many of the examples of sportsmanship featured in this book occurred out of the blue, in low-profile events that would not otherwise have been noteworthy. But when John Landy set out to break his own world mile record at the Australian National Championships in Melbourne on 11 March 1956, a whole nation held its breath. Twenty-two thousand spectators were packed into the stadium, and millions more followed the race on radio or television, which was then in its infancy. If you did not own a television, you invited yourself around to a neighbour who did, or you stood outside a department store with appropriate window dressing, watching the television through the glass. One way or another, you were there.

There is no more sports-mad city on the planet than Melbourne. In Sydney and Brisbane, people take their eye off the ball and head for the beach. Melbournians never take their eye off the ball. They love a fighter. They love a winner. And they adored John Landy.

You only have to rewrite the sporting history books ever so slightly for Landy to be even more renowned than he is. If Roger Bannister had not been the first man to run the four-minute mile, the Australian – who was no less gifted and no less determined – would have achieved the feat. He came tantalisingly close, with a time of 4 minutes 2 seconds, in March 1954. After Bannister went through the four-minute barrier in May of the same year, Landy broke his record a few weeks later, at an event in Finland, to become the fastest miler in history, at 3 minutes 58 seconds.

The sporting world was captivated by the rivalry between two athletes from opposite ends of the planet pursuing the same goal. When Bannister and Landy finally met head-to-head, in the British Empire Games in Vancouver in August 1954, it was dubbed The Race of the Century and The Miracle Mile. Bannister won by a whisker, passing Landy on the final bend; but it was the Australian who remained the world record-holder.

Nobody knew it at the time, but Landy was carrying an injury in Vancouver. Unable to sleep the night before the race, he was wandering the streets barefoot at 3 a.m. when he gashed his foot on a flashbulb discarded by a photographer. The wound required four stitches, and was still seeping blood during the race, but Landy swore the doctor to secrecy. The episode was typical of a private, undemonstrative man who shunned the limelight whenever possible.

At the 1956 National Championships in Melbourne, Landy was gunning for his own world record. And not too many people were betting against him.

But the sporting gods had something else in store: an anti-climax, but an anti-climax tinged with a glory that no climax could match.

Halfway through the race, with the runners bunched together, Ron Clarke – a great distance runner in his own right – was heading the pack when he stumbled after clipping another athlete's heels. Landy desperately tried to hurdle him, but his spikes landed on Clarke's arm. As the other runners streamed past, Landy stopped, turned and trotted back to Clarke to check that he was all right. Then he apologised and helped him to his feet. Only then, having lost precious seconds, did he continue running.

With a lap and a half to go, Landy still had time, just, to catch up the rest of the field, which he duly did, roared on by the crowd, winning the race in 4 minutes 4 seconds – just six seconds outside the world record. How long had he wasted helping Clarke back to his feet? Eight seconds? Ten seconds? For the statisticians, it was a day of what-ifs and might-have-beens. For others, including journalist Harry Gordon, writing in the *Sun News-Pictorial*, it was something else.

'It was a senseless piece of chivalry,' he declared, 'but it will be remembered as one of the finest actions in the history of sport.'

Senseless chivalry, indeed. In an exquisite oxymoron, Gordon had put his finger on the very essence of sportsmanship. Yes, Landy could have done the sensible thing: ignored his fallen rival, carried on running, beaten the world record. Instead, sublimely, he let his heart rule his head.

The Reverend Alan Moyes, who was there in the stadium, had a similar reaction to Gordon: 'It was the most incredibly stupid, beautiful, foolish, gentlemanly act I have ever seen.' The halo-polishing had begun.

The sad thing about the Landy–Clarke incident is how little satisfaction it has given the man at the centre of it. With sportsmanship, almost invariably, goes modesty. A top athlete is under severe pressure already: pressure to win; pressure to meet the expectations of adoring fans. The last thing he needs is to be regarded as a walking saint.

Even as the plaudits rang in his ears, Landy was revolting against his lionisation by the press. He wanted to get on with his job: training, competing, targeting new records. He had no stomach for celebrity, particularly the kind of celebrity that gave him the status of a moral demi-god.

'I was very embarrassed and upset about the whole thing,' he told an interviewer from the *Sydney Morning Herald* in 2004, nearly fifty years after the event. 'I still am. I wish it had never happened.'

Asked why, he replied: 'Simply because I think sport is about winning and about records. It's not about those sort of things. That was a very personal business and I think it's unfortunate that such a lot is made of it.'

In an old man talking one can catch the authentic voice of the Australian sportsman through the ages: laconic, hard-bitten, unsentimental, terrified of sounding pompous or vainglorious.

Runners, by training and temperament, are among the most machine-like of sportsmen. The stopwatch rules their lives. They repeat the same physical processes again and again, striving for those tiny improvements that can lead to a world record or a personal best. 'I would rather be beaten in 3 minutes 58 than win in 4 minutes 10,' Landy once said, in a curious but revealing comment. Never was the loneliness of the long-distance runner – living in a bubble, oblivious to those around him – laid more bare. Even in a crowded field, they are on their own, absorbed in their own thought-processes.

But man, ultimately, is not a machine. The stopwatch can only control his actions so far. Even at his most robotically efficient, he is prey to outside influences. The balm of compassion can get into the machinery – as it did so memorably on this occasion.

Landy had always been a man of contradictions. As a young athlete, when he was targeting the four-minute mile, he set himself a training regime that, by the standards of the time, was quite ferocious. But when he wanted to take a break from running, he reverted to an old childhood hobby – and it is hard to think of a less ferocious one – butterfly-collecting. He rarely talked about his hobby, but it offers a telling insight into a gentle, private person.

'Do good by stealth,' urged Alexander Pope, 'and blush to find it fame.' John Landy followed the maxim to the letter. There is something poignant in the story of a decent man doing what came naturally, following his instincts – and the humanity of those instincts being revealed, to his undying embarrassment, to twenty thousand spectators.

But we should not undervalue that humanity, however much Landy might want us to. If sport is about more than entertainment, if some higher purpose is served by thousands of people gathering in the same place at the same time, to witness the unfolding drama, then this fifty-year-old fable of compassion illustrates that truth better than anything.

Mark Taylor Declares

GETTY IMAGES

And, *pace* John Landy, is sport 'all about winning and about records'? Are there not times when, for the good of sport, statistics have to be treated as an irrelevance, a distraction from the main event?

Records play an intrinsic part in sport. It is only natural to get excited when a great athlete eyes up some sporting Everest, or targets something not previously achieved. Tiger Woods' remorseless attempt to win more Majors than Jack Nicklaus – a feat deemed totally impossible when he started his career – has provided one of the most compelling sporting dramas of the age. Even at the Olympics, where taking part is supposed to matter more than winning, the setting of new records stands high on the agenda. *Citius, altius, fortius.* Swifter, higher, stronger. What is the Olympic motto but a spur to record-chasing?

But to the true sportsman, particularly in a team sport,

records are a trifle. They have their place in sport, but they are not the be-all and end-all. There are times when they need to be ignored, even treated with disdain.

When Don Bradman's all-conquering Australian team of 1948 amassed 721 runs in a single day against Essex – a record that still stands – one man refused to join in the turkey shoot. Keith Miller, the legendary all-rounder, strolled out to the wicket and deliberately got himself out first ball. The Australian did not even bother to take guard. A one-sided contest bored him. Statistics bored him. What were the trivia of cricket to a man who had served in the RAAF during the war, flying night sorties over Germany? 'Test cricket is not pressure,' he once said. 'Pressure is having a Messerschmitt up your arse.'

There has never been a sportsman with such a genius for puncturing the pomposities of sport. Another great Keith Miller story involves Laker's Match at Old Trafford in 1956, when the Australians were skittled on a turning pitch and went down to a crushing defeat. Between innings, Ian Johnson, the Australian captain, tried to rally his team in the dressing room with a Churchillian pep talk. 'We can fight back. We need guts and determination. We can still save this match.' Miller glanced up from the racing pages of his paper and muttered: 'Bet you 6/4 we can't.'

Whatever the game, whatever the situation, professional sportsmen are least impressive when they lose their sense of perspective; forget that, however much they crave sporting success, success counts for very little in the context of life as a whole. Conversely, they are most impressive when they retain their perspective; greet victory with a modest shrug, defeat with a wry smile.

To see immortality beckoning – even if it is only the immortality of a place in the record books – but be able, on the verge of that immortality, to step back and see the bigger picture, is the mark of the true sportsman.

No post-war Australian cricket captain has achieved greater popularity than Mark 'Tubby' Taylor – a genial, self-effacing man whose finest hour came in a Test match against Pakistan in Peshawar in 1998.

He had batted for two days and, by close of play on the second day, reached 334, equalling the highest-ever Test score by an Australian batsman, set by the great Don Bradman. It was a record that had stood for more than fifty years, and was familiar to every Australian schoolboy who had ever held a cricket bat.

Overnight, there was speculation that Taylor would not just overtake the Don, but go on to pass Brian Lara's 375, then the record Test score. A big crowd turned up the next morning, expecting him to continue his innings. But Taylor, more interested in pressing for an Australian victory than chasing personal milestones, declared the innings closed at the overnight score.

'It's the only way I will ever be bracketed with Don Bradman,' he joked, winning far more friends than if he had scored the extra run.

It was a typically modest gesture by one of the gentlemen of cricket.

A few years later, another Australian left-hander, Matthew Hayden, bludgeoned his way past Bradman's record against a toothless Zimbabwe attack, then went on to score 380, overtaking Brian Lara's 375 in the process. Never did record-chasing seem more academic, more meaningless. On a flat track, against feeble bowling, the feat induced more yawning than clapping. When Lara reclaimed the record a few months later, scoring 400 against England in Antigua, the cricketing world heaved a sigh of relief. At least Lara had scored his runs the hard way, against an attack comprising Harmison, Flintoff and Hoggard. He belonged at the top of the pile, in a way Hayden did not.

As Mark Taylor instinctively realised in Peshawar, records are just numbers on a page. It is the grace notes, the flashes of underlying humanity, that make professional sport so enthralling.

Incidentally, while the true sportsman sometimes hesitates before bagging records for himself, there can be something rather touching in him bending over backwards to help an *opponent* bag a record.

A 2008 county championship match between Somerset and Surrey at Taunton threw up a textbook example. The game was petering out into a soggy draw, in front of the proverbial two men and a dog. Only two issues remained to be settled. One, would Surrey reach the 400 they needed to get a bonus batting point? Answer: yes, when Mark Ramprakash, batting with the No. 11, Pedro Collins, carted a couple of sixes into the crowd. Two, would Ramprakash reach his double century? Answer: no. When Surrey reached the 400 mark, he was left on 199 not out. Shrugging, the former *Strictly Come Dancing* winner tucked his bat under his arm and looked around for a Somerset hand or two to shake.

Enter Justin Langer, the Somerset captain, one of those hard-as-nails Australian cricketers whose idea of a good day at the office is grinding Pommie noses in the dirt. Ambushed, untypically, by sentimentality, he gestured to Ramprakash that, as there were still a few minutes of playing time available, it would be all right for him to bat on and score the extra run he needed to get his double century. One ball should do it, thought Langer. In fact, the

Australian motioned to his fielders to drop back so that one ball would do it. Ramprakash, gratefully, took guard and prepared to prod a single.

Alas, as so often happens in cricket, the best laid plans of mice and men . . .

The bowler, Peter Trego, off-message completely, refused to give Ramprakash a cheap single. He collected his defensive push, tried to throw the stumps down and nearly ran him out – not in the script. It was now the end of the over, which meant that the other batsman, Pedro Collins, had to take a single, giving Ramprakash back the strike, allowing the other bowler, Charl Willoughby, to do the necessary. Unfortunately, Willoughby was also off-message, sending down a bouncer that soared high over the batsman's head.

Ramprakash got his 200 in the end, but only after a ludicrous, faintly embarrassing passage of play. Still, farce or no farce, all credit to Justin Langer. And all credit to cricket, too. How many other high-profile sports would have tolerated such a lapse into generosity?

Ted Williams Shows His Class

Rude. Graceless. Arrogant. Foul-mouthed. Short-tempered. Stubborn as a mule. A loner. A bigmouth. A seething mass of paranoia. The kind of man who could start a fight in an empty room.

Nothing in the life of baseball legend Ted Williams says 'sportsman'. The man may have been a giant of his sport, and a war hero to boot, but at times he could be a moral pygmy. A tragic figure, you might say, but with a lingering question mark: was he big enough to qualify as tragic?

'Babe Ruth could spit further than Ted Williams can hit a ball,' wrote a columnist in the *Boston Record* in 1956 – a reference to Williams' habit, when riled, of directing a volley of spit at fans.

In Leigh Montville's gripping biography of Williams, it is often the words that are left out that are most expressive. Here is Williams playing for the Boston Red Sox in 1950. He has had a poor game and been booed by a section of the fans: 'I don't mind the errors,' he tells reporters after the game, 'but those ****** ****** fans, they can ****** ****** ****** and you can quote me in all the papers. They're ****** ******.'

If a few expletives are neither here nor there, some of the other stories Montville tells present Williams in a much darker light. In 1949, when his first daughter, Bobby-Jo, was born, he was off fishing in Florida. Reporters rang him with the good news. There was a general expectation that he would return to Boston. Williams just carried on fishing. Williams would be similarly absent when his other two children were born.

His love-hate relationship with Red Sox fans was typical of the man. With his natural gifts, and his flair for hitting steepling home runs, Williams enjoyed folk-hero status in the bleachers. The Kid. Teddy Ballgame. The Thumper. The Splendid Splinter. His nicknames hint at the affection in which he was held. But did he reciprocate that affection? No way. In fact, it became a point of pride with him not to reciprocate it. Throughout his career, with an obstinacy that became notorious, he refused to doff his cap to fans – as prescribed by long baseball tradition – when completing a home run. Imagine Kevin Pietersen scoring a century, receiving a standing ovation, but not raising his bat. You can't do it. But that was Ted Williams in one. A genius at what he did best, but as awkward, cussed a so-and-so as ever picked up a baseball bat.

Like other large, complex personalities, he had redeeming features, quite a few of them. He did a lot of unobtrusive charity work. He championed the cause of black baseball players at a time when it was radical to do so. But as an icon of good sportsmanship, Ted Williams never stepped up to the plate.

Except maybe once.

There is a little story from the twilight of his career which shows him at his best. It takes place off the field, which marks it out from most of the other episodes in this book. But does it show Ted Williams as a model sportsman? I would like to think so. Suddenly you can see the residual kindness behind the gruff exterior. Suddenly, in a simple gesture, you can see a generosity of outlook of which very few professional sportsmen are capable.

At issue was that bane of so much professional sport – money.

The malign effect of money on sport is a subject for another book. One could argue that the role played by money in sport has been exaggerated, but there is no question that professionalism has affected the way in which sportsmen and women conduct themselves on the field. They are playing for much higher stakes. They stand to win much more – or lose much more – than a trophy on their mantelpiece. Nobody expects them to perform for peanuts, but the simple fact of their *not* playing for peanuts has cast a long shadow over sport. It is quite possible to earn large sums of money and still be a model sportsman, but it is a delicate balancing act, requiring unusual maturity.

As soon as professional sportsmen are perceived as greedy, grasping, hired mercenaries, they are damaged goods. If they can find small ways of demonstrating that money comes second, that what chiefly motivates them is their joy in playing the game, their reputation is secure. They will retire with a healthy bank balance and, however many millions they have earned, be remembered as 'true servants of the game'.

One of the earliest professional sportsmen – in the sense

that he made a fortune on the back of his sporting prowess – was William Marshal, 1st Earl of Pembroke, nonpareil of knightly valour in the Age of Chivalry. Marshal (1146–1219) and his fellow knights earned their spurs in tournaments at which the object of the exercise was to capture other knights and hold them to ransom. After becoming one of the wealthiest men in England, Marshal boasted on his deathbed of having taken more than five hundred knights prisoner in this way. But he was no cynical profiteer. After one tournament in France, in a much-admired gesture, he freed his captives without demanding any reward at all. Even then, it would seem, the true sportsman did not milk his sport for all it was worth. It was not appropriate. It was not chivalrous.

Earlier in the book I found space for David Beckham, one of the richest sportsmen in the world, who conducted himself impeccably after getting sent off against Argentina in the 1998 World Cup. Kim Nielsen, the Danish referee who showed Beckham the red card that day, also deserves an honorary mention.

I have a friend, Matt, who turns out for a Bath pub side which has an annual fixture against a Danish team. At the start of the 2008 fixture, played in Denmark, the Bath players were astonished to find that the man with the whistle looked vaguely familiar.

'How did you get *him*?' they whispered to their opponents.

'We had heard that Kim Nielsen lived near here, so we thought why not ask him, for a bit of fun? He could only say no. He said he would be delighted – and his fee was thirty euros.'

Thirty euros! The next time Premier League managers are spitting bile at referees, they should remember that figure. One of the best in the business, who only retired in 2006, was prepared to offer his services on a Sunday afternoon for the cost of a few beers. After the match, Nielsen happily posed for photos, brandishing red cards at Bath players. There was – of course – no charge.

Nielsen had no reason to feel any particular love for England or English footballers; quite the reverse. He was vilified in some sections of the English press after sending off Beckham in 1998; vilified again in 2005, after sending off Wayne Rooney in a Champions League match for sarcastically clapping in his face. But he loved football too much to exploit it for commercial gain. He preferred the values of the Age of Chivalry.

The financial chivalry which Ted Williams demonstrated was of a similar order.

In the 1959 season, largely because of a neck injury, he had had a shocker. He averaged .254 and hit just ten homers – the figures of a baseballing journeyman. From his zenith in 1941, when his average of .406 remains unequalled to this day, Bradmanesque in its unapproachability, he had declined to a point where even some of his biggest fans were begging him to retire. Williams wanted to soldier on. He had a notable landmark – five hundred career home runs – in his sights, tantalisingly close, just eight away. But he felt he had let the Red Sox down. He wanted to redeem himself. But how?

In January 1960 he appeared in the office of Dick O'Connell, the Red Sox business manager, for the usual start-of-year contract-signing, and, to the astonishment of O'Connell, proposed a pay cut. He had been paid $125,000 in 1959, the highest salary in baseball, but, as he saw it, had not played like the highest paid player in baseball. The Red

Sox could take back $35,000 for 1960. He would work for $90,000. Was that fair?

O'Connell tried to talk him out of the idea, but Williams was insistent. That was the new contract. $90,000. More than a 25 per cent pay cut.

'I don't think that will ever happen again,' O'Connell said, years later, when he carried the bruises of a thousand subsequent contract negotiations. 'Nowadays, if you want to cut a salary, the players' association is ready to take you to court.'

'I was surprised at first and later I wasn't,' said Red Sox owner Tom Yawkey. 'You have to know Ted. He's an unusual person. He does what he wants and doesn't give a damn what other people think.'

Thirty-five thousand dollars. Small bucks today. A junior squad player at the Red Sox probably earns that in a week. But in the venal world of modern sport the figure somehow seems larger, not smaller, than it did at the time. Larger because of the moral integrity it implies. Larger because, in taking a pay cut, Ted Williams had honoured the unspoken compact between a sporting hero and his fans. *If you pay to see me, I'll play my heart out for you. If I let you down, I won't make excuses, I'll accept responsibility.*

One of the saddest aspects of top-flight professional sport is the economic gulf that now exists between players and fans. At the start of the 2008–9 Premier League season, with the credit crunch starting to bite, the swanky new cars in which Manchester United players turned up for training, as reported in the *Daily Telegraph*, might have been spaceships from Mars, they stood out so starkly from their surroundings. Rio Ferdinand in a Silver Mercedes (£104,000), Wes Brown in a Porsche 911 Turbo (£100,000), Carlos Tevez in a Bentley Continental (£120,000) . . . Every nought felt like a slap in the face.

It is their money. They have earned it in a free market-place. They can spend it how they want. But it is hard not to cast a wistful eye back to the Manchester United of the 1960s, when players still took the bus to the ground and the young George Best lodged in digs in Chorlton, playing crib for a few pennies with his fellow lodgers. The players were not just in Manchester, they were *of* Manchester.

Ted Williams, allowing for inflation, was a multi-mil-lionaire in modern terms. But, as this story shows, he kept his feet firmly on the ground. It was a matter of pride with him – a point of honour – to give value for money to the club he had served with such distinction.

Surprise plot twists are the essence of sport, and this was a plot twist and a half. From a man with the natural warmth of a puff adder had come a gesture of touching generosity.

Tom Richards: Rugby's First Troubadour

The very word 'mercenary' has such derogatory connotations that the player who switches sides, for whatever reason, is one of the most reviled figures in sport. A player can earn silly money and not be resented by fans but, as soon as he transfers his allegiance from one team to another, he unleashes tribal furies.

The venom that is still directed at footballer Ashley Cole for moving from Arsenal to Chelsea has an irrational, primitive savagery. And Cole was only moving a few miles across London on a pay rise. When cricketer Kevin Pietersen, born in South Africa, elected to play for England, the possession of a unimpeachably English mother – from Canterbury, which is about as English as England gets – was not enough to save him from the South African boo mob.

The good sportsman, by definition, does not let money

sully his conduct. His guiding light is the love of the game. As for tribal loyalties, he respects them, but is not ruled by them. He is more an internationalist than a nationalist. To be born in one country, but represent another, can seem like the ultimate betrayal. It can also, in some circumstances, be the ultimate expression of sportsmanship.

There used to be a short section in *Wisden* devoted to cricketers who had played for more than one country. W. E. Midwinter, A. E. Trott, J. J. Ferris, S. M. J. Woods, F. Hearne . . . It was not a roll call of traitors but of sportsmen who, in the age before jet travel, had lived interesting lives. You wanted to know more about them. Did they experience any sense of divided loyalties? Or were they simply the cricketing equivalent of strolling players, welcome wherever they went?

C. T. B. Turner represented only one country, Australia, but his story shines like a beacon from the pages of *Wisden*. He was playing against England in Sydney in 1887 when an injury to one of the England fielders necessitated the use of a substitute. There was no England player available, so Turner sportingly made up the numbers – then took a superb catch to dismiss an Australian batsman who was well set. England went on to win the match by seventy-one runs. It is the sort of thing that goes on the whole time in village-green cricket. But this was the Ashes, one of the biggest events in sport. The Turner catch, and the sporting spirit it symbolises, added more to the mystique of the event than a dozen dreary centuries.

In football, the England centre forward Stan Mortensen – best known for scoring a hat-trick in the 'Matthews' FA Cup Final in 1953 – added to the sum of sporting trivia in his very first international. He turned out for Wales in a wartime match at Wembley in 1943. There were not enough

Welsh players available, so Mortensen got the nod. Nobody complained. Nobody accused him of treachery. It seemed the natural, sporting thing to do.

Of all the sportsmen who, for different reasons, have represented more than one country, the Australian-born rugby union player Tom 'Rusty' Richards has to be the most intriguing. He is the only man to have played for both the Wallabies and the British Lions and, appropriately, is commemorated in the Tom Richards Trophy for which the two countries compete. For a man who died more than seventy years ago, he remains extraordinarily vivid. Every detail of his short, action-packed life endears you to the man.

He was born in 1882 in Vegetable Creek, New South Wales, then moved to Charters Towers in Queensland, a gold-rush town where his father, who had emigrated to Australia from England, was hoping to make his fortune. As a sports-mad schoolboy, Tom saw rugby as a chance to escape the back-breaking life of the goldfields. He ran to develop his strength, got his younger brother to punch him non-stop to build up his abdominal muscles, then practised his tackling by catching fowls in the backyard. The magic of sport! If they made a movie of his life, half the characters would be chickens.

With that kind of superhuman dedication it was only a matter of time before his prowess as a marauding loose forward was recognised. Richards was selected for Queensland and, after a period in South Africa, prospecting for gold with his father, was part of the Wallabies team that toured Britain in 1908 and won the gold medal at the London Olympics, when Richards scored a try in the final. *The Times*, not normally given to hyperbole, was gushing in its praise: 'If ever the Earth had to select a rugby union team to play against Mars, Tom Richards would be the first player selected.'

After the Olympics, he returned to South Africa to work in the mines, but the lure of rugby was too strong. The British Lions, touring South Africa in 1910, were short of players because of injuries, so they approached Richards. Would he be willing to play for them? He had once played club rugby in England, so was technically eligible for selection.

It must have been quite a moment, a sporting life at the crossroads. In 1906, during his first stint working in South Africa, Richards had played two matches for Transvaal in the Currie Cup, but was not allowed to play for the Springboks as he had not lived in the country long enough. Turning out for the British Isles was problematic. Imagine the furore there would be today if an injury-depleted Lions team called on the services of an Australian player. There would probably be jeering from the stands.

In less sanctimonious times, Richards simply did what must have seemed the gallant, sporting thing. He donned the Lions shirt and helped them to a famous victory against the Springboks in Port Elizabeth. Then it was back to Australia, a spell with the Manly club in Sydney, the vice-captaincy of the Wallabies on a tour of the USA and Canada then, with Europe on the brink of war, a season with the French club Toulouse, whom he led to the championship.

It was the kind of itinerant sporting life that is commonplace today but, in the Edwardian era, must have seemed innovative, even revolutionary: the sportsman as missionary, gipsy, troubadour. To have represented two different countries did not make Tom Richards a turncoat: it was a natural by-product of an outgoing life, infused with the spirit of sport.

When war broke out in Europe, Richards joined the 1st Australian Division, was one of the first off the boats at

Gallipoli and later fought in France, where he won the Military Cross for gallantry. The lessons of the rugby field – courage, comradeship – had not been forgotten. But there was to be no happy homecoming for the golden boy of Australian rugby. After being gassed in the trenches, Richards suffered poor health for the rest of his life. He was just forty-six when he died.

The boy who tackled chickens was not destined to become an elder statesman of his sport. But, thanks to the Tom Richards Trophy, his name is an enduring emblem of the sportsmanship that transcends national boundaries.

John Gerber: When Not to Read a Letter

'You're a che—' There is no need to finish the sentence. In any sport, at any time, in any country, the c-word is a nuclear weapon: devastating in its impact and, once launched, impossible to recall. Accuse a fellow sportsman of cheating and you will make an enemy for life.

Cheating is as old as sport and, in many sports, perceptions of what constitutes cheating have changed over the years. But the one thing that has never changed is the explosive power of the word. Its deployment on the field has provoked flash point after flash point. Remember England cricket captain Mike Gatting squaring up to umpire Shakoor Rana on the 1987 tour of Pakistan? Gatting thought he had been called a cheat. In 2006, in a Test between the same two countries at the Oval, it was the turn of the Pakistani captain, Inzamam-ul-Haq, to lose his rag with Australian umpire Darrell Hair. Inzamam thought his team had been accused of cheating, by tampering with the ball, and refused to lead them out on to the field after tea. The honour of his country, as he saw it, had been impugned.

Good sportsmen, it goes without saying, never cheat. But they are sensitive to what you might call the etiquette of name calling. A sporting competitor does not lightly accuse his opponent of cheating. He weighs the evidence, chooses his words with care; he gives his opponent the benefit of the doubt; he avoids unnecessary, acrimonious, friendship-ending confrontations.

A fine example of a potentially explosive situation defused by the tact and sensitivity of those involved occurred in Italy in 1963. The sport was bridge, and the match, between Italy and the United States, was the Bermuda Bowl, the equivalent of the World Cup Final.

The protagonists of the story, both now dead, were the non-playing captains of the respective teams: Carl'Alberto Perroux of Italy, a criminal lawyer by trade, and America's John Gerber, who gave his name to a bidding convention which is still in use. Golfers ask each other: 'What's your handicap?' Bridge players ask each other: 'Do you play Gerber or Roman key card Blackwood?' In the madhouse of sport, lunacy takes many forms.

Bridge may seem like a sedate pastime, but, as anyone who has ever played the game will testify, it can descend into bickering in a matter of seconds. Adultery aside, there is probably no other indoor pastime that has put the skids under so many marriages. And in the nature of the game, the scope for cheating is almost limitless.

Just think of those 'friendly' games of bridge around the kitchen table. If you can peep over Uncle Ron's shoulder while he is refilling his wine glass, you are ahead of the game. And the same temptations are present, for obvious reasons, at top-flight bridge, with big sums of money at stake.

If you know that your partner holds, say, the ace of diamonds, you have got a big advantage over your opponents. And if your partner can signal possession of the ace of diamonds by some cunning pre-arranged signal – scratching his nose with the little finger of his left hand, say – the subterfuge can be very hard to detect.

At the time of the 1963 Bermuda Bowl, cheating in bridge, though hardly unprecedented, had yet to cause a major scandal in an international event. But the spectre was waiting in the wings. Rumours of cheating were two a penny, and a fair few of those rumours, absurd or not so absurd, centred on the Italian team captained by Carl'Alberto Perroux.

Known universally as the Blue Team, it was the most gifted and innovative combination of players in the history of the game – as hallowed, in its way, as the 1970 Brazil football team or the West Indies cricket teams of the early 1980s. Players like Giorgio Belladonna and Benito Garozzo pulled off such spectacular coups at the table that other players started to talk. Were they as brilliant as they seemed? Or was there some funny business going on?

It was a time for cool heads and kind hearts.

On the eve of the Bermuda Bowl, an anonymous letter, written in Italian, was delivered to John Gerber at the hotel where the two teams were staying. Gerber asked for a translator to read it out. The contents were so potentially inflammatory that, after hearing just one paragraph, Gerber told the translator to stop. He then had the letter sent to Perroux, inviting his comments, and explaining that he had not read the whole letter. The Italian, after reading the letter aloud to his team – it did indeed contain accusations of cheating – suggested to Gerber that, in order to preserve the integrity of the event, and remove any suggestion of foul play, the match should be played with screens separating the players, to prevent partners exchanging coded signals with each other. Gerber, in the same conciliatory spirit, rejected the offer. What was any game worth if the opposing teams could not trust each other?

After the match, which Italy won, the Italian players were

so grateful to Gerber for the diplomatic way he had handled the accusations of cheating that they gave their trophies to their American opponents.

The story is often cited as the finest example of sportsmanship in bridge. Sadly, it was to be one of the last. Just two years later, in one of the most notorious scandals in sporting history, two English players, Terence Reese and Boris Schapiro, were found guilty of cheating at a tournament in Buenos Aires, using hand signals to convey information about the cards they held. They protested their innocence, but some of the evidence against them was damning. Gerber found himself, in effect, a witness for the prosecution. Perroux, sitting on the panel adjudicating the matter, abstained.

The age of card-playing innocence was dead. In 1975, two members of the Italian Blue Team were reprimanded after exchanging information by means of foot signals under the table. Wooden screens separating the players – as proposed by Perroux in 1963 – were introduced and are now the norm in major international events. The screens may have reduced the possibility of cheating, but what a sad indictment of bridge and those who play it at the highest level!

That lovely, friendly card game – four players sitting around a table, able to smile at each other, swap jokes, chat between hands – now feels more like a security zone at an airport. Trust has been replaced by distrust. What happened to the spirit of 1963, when an American gentleman refused to think ill of a fellow sportsman?

Adam Gilchrist Bucks the Trend

Sydney Cricket Ground, 5 January 2003. An England bats-man nicks the ball through to Australian wicket-keeper Adam Gilchrist, who appeals for a catch. 'Not out,' says the umpire. '****!' screams Gilchrist, at the top of his voice. Welcome to professional sport in the twenty-first century. It's not pretty, but it's entertaining.

In a perfect world, that sporting Eden we all dream about, the England batsman would walk without waiting to be given out, the umpire would not be left looking like an idiot and Gilchrist's contribution to the script would not require asterisks. But nobody has done anything particularly heinous. Gilchrist swore so loudly that he ended up receiv-ing an official reprimand from the match referee. But it was a hot day and Australia, untypically, were losing a Test match. These things happen in Ashes cricket.

Matthew Hayden, one of Gilchrist's team-mates, had an

even worse sense-of-humour failure in the same match, smashing a pane in the dressing-room door and incurring a fine from the referee. In the English press there was a modicum of pious tut-tutting. Could it be that these Aussie supermen, all-conquering on the field, were bad losers? But Gilchrist himself, one of the nice guys, attracted little flak. He had over-reacted. End of story.

Nobody knew it at the time, but beneath the surface, inside the head of one of the greatest cricketers ever to grace the game, priorities were being reassessed and conventional wisdoms challenged.

Fast-forward a couple of months to Port Elizabeth in South Africa. Gilchrist is opening the batting for Australia against Sri Lanka. It is the semi-final of the World Cup, a big match, and Gilchrist has started nicely, 22 off 19 balls. Then he tries to sweep a ball, gets a bottom edge on to his pad and the ball balloons up in the air, to be caught by the wicketkeeper. '*Howzat?*' roar the Sri Lankan fielders.

Let Gilchrist himself take up the story: 'To see the umpire shaking his head, meaning "Not out", gave me the strangest feeling. I don't recall what my exact thoughts were, but somewhere in the back of my mind, all that history from the Ashes series was swirling around, all those batsmen, both in my team and against us, standing their ground . . . I had spent all summer wondering if it was possible to take ownership of those incidents and still be successful. I had wondered what I would do. And I was about to find out.

'The voice in my head was emphatic. *Go. Walk.* And I did.'

With which, to general amazement, the batsman who had just been reprieved by the umpire marched back to the dressing room without so much as a backward glance.

In the 1950s or 1960s, as cricket said its long goodbye to the amateur era, such behaviour would have been unremarkable. The overwhelming majority of batsmen 'walked' when they knew they were out: that was the prevailing ethical code. But for a professional cricketer to walk in the twenty-first century – particularly at a critical point in an important match – had something marvellously quixotic about it. To the millions watching on television, it must have felt as if the clock had been turned back to the 1930s and Jack Hobbs was at the crease.

As Gilchrist makes clear, his decision to walk was not premeditated. Like so many of the moments of sportsmanship featured in the book, it was a spur-of-the-moment gesture, born of pure impulse. 'The voice in my head was emphatic . . .' It could almost be a born-again Christian talking. But it was not totally unpremeditated. It followed a period in which a decent man had been reflecting on the sometimes fractious spirit in which professional cricket was played, and what he, Adam Gilchrist, could do to improve that spirit. He was tired of the mean-spiritedness creeping into the game and wanted to find a better way.

Back in the Australian dressing room, Gilchrist was quizzed by bemused team-mates. What was he thinking of? Hadn't he just made a free a gift to the other side? Would a Sri Lankan batsman have done the same? The inevitable questions.

Later in the same innings, one of the other Australian batsman, Michael Bevan, was mistakenly given out by the umpire, leaving Gilchrist to reflect: 'That showed perfectly why you don't walk – because you're likely to get a rotten decision like that, and you don't get to walk in reverse.' As the Australian innings closed on 212-7, well below par, he was still racked by doubts.

In the event, Australia went on to win the game, then the World Cup itself. For Gilchrist, it was the perfect win-win: a trophy plus the moral high ground. More importantly, he had made a resolution. Port Elizabeth would not be a one-off, an isolated gesture, but set the standard for the future: every time he nicked a catch, he would walk without waiting for the umpire's verdict.

And, more importantly still, he kept that resolution.

'It was a really weird situation,' Gilchrist wrote in his memoir, *Walking to Victory*, looking back on the Port Elizabeth incident. 'I was going against the grain of what 99 per cent of cricketers do these days . . . But at the end of the day, I had been honest with myself, and the more I thought about it, the more settled I became with what I had done. *You did it for the right reasons.*'

For the next five years, until his retirement, he was an Olympian figure, blazing some brilliant centuries, but also etching another image in the memory of cricket fans: the image of a great batsman nicking a ball to the wicket-keeper, then striding off the field, his bat under his arm, without hesitating, without grumbling, without even deigning to hope that the umpire would make a mistake.

'Oh, it's easy for Gilchrist,' said the cynics. He was an exceptional player in an exceptional team. As a wicket-keeper who averaged fifty in Test matches – a unique accomplishment – he never had to worry about losing his place. Someone picked for his batting alone knows that a bad run of form, compounded by umpiring mistakes going against him, can cost him his livelihood: that is how professional cricketers justify their reluctance to walk, even when they know they have hit the ball.

Certainly, although Test batsmen do sometimes walk, there has been no great rush to follow Gilchrist's example.

The great Brian Lara was an inveterate walker, but he cut almost as lonely a figure as the Australian wicket-keeper. From Karachi to Cape Town, you still see batsmen standing their ground, feigning innocence, even as the TV replay shows them nicking the ball. 'Cheats,' say the old-timers. 'Just hard-nosed professionals,' say the realists. 'They all do it, so they cancel each other out.' One way or another, the game has lost its innocence.

But the example is still there. Even now that Gilchrist has retired, the honesty he epitomised remains the template by which other cricketers will be judged. His explosive batting alone would have ensured his place in the pantheon of cricketing greats. But he has earned himself another, no less glorious memorial – a true Corinthian in an un-Corinthian age.

Jacky Ickx: Challenging the Status Quo

In Adam Gilchrist's account of his Damascene conversion to walking, one phrase stands out: the need for players to 'take ownership' of their sport, not leave things entirely to officials and TV technology.

The Australian wicket-keeper saw, with admirable clarity, that sport and trust are indissoluble. If sportsmen compete in a spirit of mutual suspicion, unwilling to deal honestly with each other, the whole mood of the occasion turns sour. Honour codes cannot be sub-contracted to officials, with their imperfect eyesight and fallible judgement: they have to be part of the unspoken compact between the competing athletes. And, as a corollary of that, officials sometimes have to be over-ruled. In sport, as in life, it is right to obey the law, but not all the time.

Another famous 'walker', in a very different sport, was the

Belgian racing driver Jacky Ickx, who took ownership of his sport in the most dramatic of fashions, forcing a long-over-due change on the regulatory body.

In Formula One, Ickx fell just short of true greatness: he never won the drivers' championship, despite twenty-five podium finishes. But at endurance racing he was an acknowledged master, winning the 24 Hours of Le Mans a record-breaking six times. The most celebrated of his wins – revolutionary in more ways than one – came in 1969, the first year he competed.

Rookie racing drivers are not meant to use their brains: they are just meant to drive like bats out of hell and add a dash of youthful recklessness to proceedings. Ickx was made of more cerebral stuff. Unintimidated by his more experienced rivals, and by the long history of the Le Mans event, which had been held since 1923, he entered the lists with one thing on his mind: to rewrite the rule book.

Traditions are integral to sport, and the 24 Hours of Le Mans, one of the biggest events in motor racing, taking place in a whirl of French flummery, is no exception. There are right ways of doing things and wrong ways of doing things. If the race takes place on the same weekend as a presidential election, for example, as it did in 1969, it starts late, to enable people to vote.

It was at Le Mans in 1967 that a racing driver, Dan Gurney, first sprayed those around the podium with champagne, a ritual that has since become obligatory. Another great Le Mans tradition is the waving of safety flags by track marshals during the final lap, congratulating the winning drivers.

Until Ickx, still in his early twenties, dared to challenge the status quo, the start of the Le Mans race was also wreathed in colourful ritual. In a tradition dating back to the

1920s, when the priority was ensuring that no driver stole an unfair advantage, cars were lined up alongside the pit wall in the order in which they qualified, with the drivers standing on the opposite side of the front stretch. When the French flag dropped to signify the start, the drivers would sprint across the track to their cars, which they would have to enter and start without assistance, before driving away. It made for great sporting theatre, with drivers hurling themselves into their cars and fumbling for their ignition keys. There was only one problem: in their scramble to make a fast getaway, many drivers omitted to fasten their seat belts, sometimes with fatal consequences.

Tragedy and Le Mans had long gone hand in hand. The most infamous accident occurred in 1955, when more than eighty spectators were killed after Pierre Levegh's Mercedes flew into the crowd. And, although new safety measures had been introduced, they fell short of what common sense – in the person of Jacky Ickx – demanded.

In 1968, one of his Belgian compatriots, Willy Mairesse, had crashed during the first lap and, because he had not yet fastened his seat belt, suffered devastating injuries. He never raced again and, a year later, took his own life. Ickx was not prepared just to follow the Le Mans traditions, lemming-like, unthinking. He had his own passionately held agenda.

Most of the instances of sportsmanship in this book were unpremeditated. Circumstances conspired to create a little moral conundrum which had to be solved in an instant: there was no time to think. Ickx, by contrast, did have time to think. Even before the race had begun, he saw exactly what was needed and, with the confidence of youth, executed it to perfection.

As the other drivers sprinted to their cars, in the time-honoured fashion, Ickx ostentatiously walked across the track. Jackie Oliver his co-driver has likened it to a Monty Python-style silly walk; others remember it as a nonchalant amble, with Ickx pretending to look for his car keys. In any event, the Belgian was so far off the pace that he was nearly hit by one of the other cars as it roared away from the grid. Ickx then got into his own car and, with the same deliberate ostentation, did up his seat belt before driving off.

It was a bold statement of intent, the message crystal-clear: this is sport, not war; nobody needs to get killed. And the message was about to be underscored in the most poignant fashion, when one of the other drivers, John Woolfe, a gentleman amateur from England, crashed on the first lap and was killed. Another driver, Chris Amon, also had to retire after an accident.

Inevitably, as a result of his protest, Ickx started at the back of the field and had to claw his way back into contention. His efforts to do so led to one of the most dramatic races in history and inspired the Steve McQueen movie *Le Mans*. The endgame featured a titanic tussle between the young Belgian, in his Gulf/Wyer GT40, and the German veteran Hans Herrmann, driving a Porsche 908 LH.

During the last hour of the race, with both drivers exhausted, but still driving flat out, in slippery conditions, the lead changed hands again and again. If Ickx had narrowly lost, he would have paid the ultimate penalty for his demonstration at the start of the race. But Fate smiled on him: he crossed the finishing line just ahead of Herrmann, writing the first chapter in a glorious sporting legend.

'One should never overestimate a victory,' Ickx once said. But it is hard to overestimate the importance of this one. Not only had a new star been born, but the gauntlet had been thrown down to the race organisers: get rid of the antiquated Le Mans start.

And the organisers, to their credit, picked up the gauntlet. The next year they made the long-overdue reform that was needed: drivers would no longer have to sprint across the grid to their cars, but start *in* their cars, wearing seat belts. Game, set and match to common sense. One very determined Belgian rookie had forced a changing of the guard.

In a surreal postscript to the 1969 race, Ickx himself was involved in a car accident the very next day. He was driving back to Paris when, near Chartres, another car pulled out in front of his Porsche, which swerved into a telegraph pole. The car was a complete write-off, but Ickx simply undid his seat belt and walked from the vehicle unharmed.

He would go on to win the 24 Hours of Le Mans on five further occasions. But nothing could ever match the theatricality of his debut. Sportsmanship and morality are intertwined, and what higher morality is there than the saving of human life? No racing driver hurtling down the home stretch stirred the imagination as much as Jacky Ickx, sauntering across the Le Mans starting grid, as if he had all the time in the world.

Sebastien Loeb: Putting the Champagne on Hold

Danger and motor sport are inseparable, and, although fatalities are far rarer than they used to be, they can still cast their grim shadow across the stage, challenging the participants to produce an appropriate response.

At the 2005 Wales Rally GB, the great French driver Sebastien Loeb, five times winner of the World Rally Drivers' Championship, had to show quick-wittedness as well as compassion.

On stage fifteen of the rally, the Peugeot driver Markko Martin crashed heavily into a tree. He was unharmed, but his co-driver, Michael 'Beef' Park, one of the great characters of the sport, sustained fatal injuries. It was the first death in a WRC event for eight years. The organisers halted the stage and abandoned the final two stages of the rally – which, in the normal course of events, would have meant that Loeb, who was leading at the time, would be declared the winner, thus clinching the drivers' championship for the year.

Luckily, the Frenchman had his wits about him. He had no desire to celebrate in such sombre circumstances, so he found an ingenious way to avoid winning the rally, deliberately incurring a two-minute time penalty by arriving early at the final checkpoint. This dropped him to third place overall and allowed Norwegian Petter Solberg, one of his main rivals for the championship, to win the rally.

'There is no way I wanted to win the world title in circumstances like that,' Loeb explained afterwards. 'Who wins the race is not what counts today.'

The Frenchman had to wait until the next event to clinch the title, but duly did so – in far happier circumstances.

In a sport where raw aggression is so often the deciding factor, his little gesture of renunciation – obvious in retrospect, but not necessarily obvious at the time – perfectly caught the mood of the hour.

Alpay Ozalan: The Defender Who Forgot to Foul*

Another footballer, another fair play award and, without wanting to be churlish, another instance of sportsmanship that is so flawed it requires an asterisk.

By the mid-1990s, cheating in football had become so endemic that the European Fair Play Movement, an off-shoot of the European Olympic Movement, came into being. Lovers of the beautiful game were desperate for a footballer to honour, to remind people that it still *was* a beautiful game; and, as Pele and Bobby Charlton had retired, they hit on the little-known Turkish defender Alpay Ozalan, giving him the inaugural EFPM Fair Play Award in 1996.

What had he done? Admitted to handling the ball in the penalty area? Come to the aid of an injured opponent? Congratulated a linesman on his excellent eyesight? Not quite. It was what he had not done which impressed the EFPM judges.

Turkey were playing Croatia at the City Ground, Nottingham, at Euro 96. The game was about to fizzle out into a uneventful draw when a Croatian forward, with Ozalan at his heels, broke clear and bore down on the Turkish goal. Any other defender in the same position as Ozalan would have committed a professional foul – the Croatian player had not even reached the penalty area, so it would have been a low-tariff offence. Instead, abjuring such cynicism, Ozalan allowed him to continue unimpeded, scoring what proved to be the winning goal.

You can see why I have insisted on putting an asterisk against Ozalan's name. What kind of sport doles out awards to players simply for not cheating? And what kind of sport dignifies cheating with the term 'professional foul', surely the most odious oxymoron in the whole sporting lexicon? If it is a foul, then it is wrong, and if it is wrong, then it is *un*-professional – certainly in the language the rest of us use. The Ozalan episode may have its own quaint charm, but it is a damning indictment of the topsy-turvy values of top-flight football.

After the match, as was sadly predictable, the player got a pasting in the Turkish press. 'He could have hung on to the Croatian's waist and prevented the goal,' declared one journalist. 'It might have been ugly, but he could even have tripped him from behind. At least we would have won a point.' A journalist on another paper was even more scathing. 'No team made up of professionals would have lost a goal like that.' That p-word again, toxic and insidious.

To rub salt in the wound, Ozalan himself, having been put on a pedestal by the EFPM, spent the rest of his career jumping off the pedestal at every opportunity. He was sent off at Euro 2000 after striking a Portuguese player and sent off again in the 2006 World Cup after pulling a Brazilian player back by the shirt. Other low points in his career included poking a finger in David Beckham's face during a match in Istanbul, kicking out at a Swiss defender during a scuffle in a tunnel, and getting involved in a punch-up with team-mate Juan Pablo Angel during his spell at Aston Villa.

But, again, as with the Robbie Fowler penalty, an isolated good deed, flawed once it is subjected to scrutiny, is not without iconic value.

In sport, as in life, there can be a quiet kind of heroism in not following the herd. Simply by not doing something wrong, when it has become normal practice, one is making a statement. On the Bodyline tour of Australia, Gubby Allen famously refused to adopt the tactics being deployed by the other England fast bowlers – he regarded them as objectionable, so he took a firm moral stance. The restraint exercised by Alpay Ozalan was on a smaller scale, but similar in nature.

The image of a forward bearing down on goal with the ball at his feet, everyone assuming he will be fouled, then the foul not happening, has the joy of the unexpected about it, an escape from the dour realities of professional football into a better world. In fantasy football, the game of all our dreams, there are no professional fouls. Every match ends 5-4, or 9-8, with the winning goal scored by the young George Best, dancing through tackles, as free as air.

So two cheers for Alpay Ozalan for supplying us with that image. We need to hold on to it.

Boris Spassky: A Warm Man in a Cold War

Sporting chivalry may enchant us, make us smile, even bring a tear to our eyes. But when, in the wider scheme of things, did an act of sportsmanship ever change anything?

Take a bow, Boris Vasilievich Spassky.

Several books have been written about the famous showdown between Spassky and Bobby Fischer in Reykjavik in 1972 – East versus West at the height of the Cold War, with a chessboard as the battleground and the world championship at stake. Many more books have been written about the Cold War itself. The Spassky–Fischer match was an event of such huge symbolic significance that it is impossible to do it justice in a general book of this kind. But one feature of the match is surely worth underscoring: the good sportsmanship shown by the Russian player, and the impact of that sportsmanship on the wider world.

It may be a cliché to talk of sportsmen as ambassadors for their countries, but it is a cliché with a large grain of truth. In Portugal recently I was asked by my hosts what the British thought of the Portuguese. I shuffled in embarrassment. The fact was, I said, and I was only half-joking, that our recent perceptions of Portugal had been shaped by two high-profile Portuguese stars with oversize egos: Cristiano Ronaldo and José Mourinho. Portuguese beaches had a good reputation. There were said to be some excellent restaurants in Lisbon. But one did not come to Portugal and expect to find humility.

Russia in 1972 – and it was only four years since Russian tanks had rolled into Czechoslovakia – had an even worse image problem. There was the odd crack in the wall. That very same summer, at the Munich Olympics, teenage Russian gymnast Olga Korbut had charmed the world with her gap-toothed smile. But a wall it was, and a wall that had been there for as long as most of us could remember. However much you try to judge countries by their people, not their political systems, it is easier said than done, particularly when a political system is cold, monolithic, totalitarian.

We had all heard about the famous Russian soul. We knew about the Russia of Tolstoy and Tchaikovsky and Chekhov and those elegant conversations by the samovar. But how much of that Russia had survived half a century of communism? It seemed such a grey place, run by faceless apparatchiks, inhabited by misery guts who looked as if they had forgotten how to smile, or had never learnt. Better Uncle Sam any day, warts and all.

As Spassky and Fischer did battle over the chessboard, with the eyes of the world upon them, those cultural preconceptions came under the microscope and, little by tiny little, started to change.

In all great sporting encounters one can discern two

separate, subsidiary battles taking place in tandem with the contest itself. One is the battle for psychological advantage. The other is the battle for the moral high ground. It is perfectly possible to win one battle and lose the other. A boxer who racially abused his opponent might unsettle him, thus gaining the upper hand psychologically; but he would forfeit the moral respect of neutrals. In cricket, the fielding side might sledge a batsman out, but if their sledging were gratuitously insulting, they would surrender the moral high ground. The jockeying for position in the various mind-games can be as fascinating as the match itself. It certainly was in Reykjavik.

There were so much behind-the-scenes gamesmanship and counter-gamesmanship that it was hard to concentrate on the chess. The loose cannon was the psychotically insecure, egotistical genius that was Bobby Fischer. He lost the first game, sulked, failed to turn up for the second game, forfeited it, then demanded that the third game be played in a small separate room, not the main hall. Spassky, instead of telling the American to get lost, agreed. His gesture was the height of the magnanimity – he was defending champion, so he could simply have walked away and retained his crown – but got scant reward.

Fischer – after more outrageous behaviour before the game, when he prowled around the room inspecting the remote-control cameras – suddenly started to show signs of the mercurial brilliance that made him one of the greatest chess players of all time. He won the game and, psychologically, had gained a decisive advantage. The momentum was with him, and stayed with him.

As the match unfolded, one thing was becoming crystal-clear to the millions following it – who included myself, a chess-mad schoolboy in Surrey.

The American was the better chess player, but the Russian was the better man.

It was a simplistic conclusion, perhaps, but because it contradicted the equally simplistic assumptions of the Cold War, in which *we* were the good guys, it was a simplistic conclusion with profound implications. In the good sportsmanship of one man, the whole of Russia, the whole of the Soviet Union, had suddenly assumed a much friendlier demeanour. That little man in a grey suit – a bit stiff in manner, perhaps, but as we slowly got to know him, possessed of a quiet, impressive humanity – was a harbinger of better times ahead.

Boris Spassky held no brief for Communism. His embarrassment at the political circus of Reykjavik – with the whole Soviet machine willing him towards victory and Henry Kissinger getting involved on the American side – was obvious. He detested the Soviet system and would later emigrate to France. But he was a Russian patriot and, in his gentlemanly demeanour at the chessboard, under the severest provocation, he did his country proud.

His finest hour – as a man, not as a chess player – came in the sixth game. The match was tied at 2½ -2½ when Fischer, playing white, caught his opponent off-guard with an unexpected opening, then followed up with masterly attacking play, forcing the Russian to resign. As the crowd burst out clapping, Spassky, the soul of chivalry, joined in the applause.

Would Bobby Fischer have applauded if the positions had been reversed? It was inconceivable. He had the innate smallness of all men with large egos. The match, and the kudos, would be his. But the moral high ground, and everything that signified in a world divided by ideology, belonged to the Russian, a true sporting ambassador for his country.

*

Once a sportsman, always a sportsman, and in the case of Boris Spassky, there was to be a glorious coda to the Reykjavik match, more than thirty years later.

He and Bobby Fischer had gone their very separate ways. Fischer, more impossible and temperamental by the day, became a virtual recluse. Spassky carried stolidly on where he had left off: a fine chess player but never, quite, a genius. Then, in 1992, by which time Spassky was living in France, the two men staged a twentieth-anniversary rematch in Montenegro and Belgrade, then part of Yugoslavia. Fischer won, as he had in Reykjavik.

Spassky's participation in the match was relatively uncontentious but, because Yugoslavia was subject to UN sanctions, Fischer faced the wrath of the US authorities. He had been warned against taking part in the match by the State Department, which now issued a warrant for his arrest. For a period, Fischer became a stateless nomad, living in Hungary and the Philippines and issuing the odd rabidly anti-American statement, usually with a poisonous anti-Semitic subtext, particularly in the wake of 9/11. Then, in 2004, he was arrested by immigration authorities in Japan while using a revoked US passport, then detained under threat of extradition to the States.

It was too much for Spassky, who was so appalled by the way his rival had been treated that, in July 2004, he wrote an open letter to President George W. Bush. It is a marvellous, heart-warming document: profound in its generosity, but also laced with humour. The fact that it was penned by someone whose first language was not English, which accounts for the odd clumsy phrase, only makes it more touching. You can almost hear Spassky, white knight of chess, in full emotional spate.

'Bobby is a tragic personality,' the Russian concluded his

letter. 'I realised that at the time. He is an honest and good-natured man. Absolutely not social. He is not adaptable to everyone's standards of life. He has a very high sense of justice and is unwilling to compromise as well as with his own conscience as with surrounding people. He is a person who is doing almost everything against himself.

'I would not like to defend or justify Bobby Fischer. He is what he is. I am asking only for one thing. For mercy, charity.

'If for some reason it is impossible, I would like to ask you the following. Bobby and myself committed the same crime. Put sanctions against me also. Arrest me. And put me in the same cell as Bobby Fischer. And give us a chess set.'

Bravo! Was any letter written by a sportsman so worthy of a standing ovation?

In terms of influencing President Bush, it was a waste of time. The words 'pearls' and 'swine' come to mind. Bobby Fischer never returned to the United States and eventually settled in Iceland, where he died in 2008.

But for Boris Vasilievich Spassky – a gentleman at the chessboard and a big-hearted human being, without malice or pettiness – it is impossible to feel anything but admiration.

Michal Krissak: Orphan and Hero

If the instinct to act sportingly is universal, the courage to follow that instinct, particularly during a big match, is much rarer. One sometimes reads the obituary of a VC holder who protested to his dying day that he had no choice: he just did what came naturally, what the circumstances of battle demanded. And one thinks, no, he did have a choice; if he had not taken a course of action which, to his fellow soldiers, seemed exceptional, out of the ordinary, beyond the call of duty, he would not have been recommended for a VC in the first place.

It is the same with sportsmanship. There might be eleven players in a team but, when push comes to shove, only one of the eleven who is prepared to do the decent thing; make the selfless sporting gesture which the fans remember.

In 1999, when Slovak mountaineer Michal Krissak saw a fellow climber lying face down in the snow on Mount McKinley in Alaska, his first instinct was to go to his aid. For twenty-one-year-old Krissak it was the natural, obvious, inescapable thing to do. But it was not so obvious to the other climbers on the mountain, who simply left the man to his fate. It was nine in the evening, night was falling and, at 19,500 feet, where the body was lying, the temperature was 25 degrees Fahrenheit and falling. The warmth of the base camp beckoned.

As Krissak, who had just completed a solo ascent of the

mountain, approached the motionless body, he saw a group of five men standing around it. Instead of offering help, they headed down the mountain, leaving the Slovak to deal with the situation on his own. The man – a Japanese climber called Shigeo Tamoi – was semi-conscious, and Krissak had to slap his face hard to revive him. Tamoi eventually came to, but his water bottle was empty and he had no survival gear.

Krissak held him by his shoulders and the two men slowly descended together. Another group of climbers – three this time – saw them, ignored them and hurried past. Krissak called out and asked if they had any water. Still they took no notice. An incredulous Krissak had to threaten one of them physically, shaking him by the shoulders, until he got the water he needed.

When they reached the 18,200-foot Denali Pass, a three-man American team spurned Krissak's request to let Tamoi tie on to their rope for the hazardous thousand-foot descent to West Buttress high camp. The men said they were cold and needed to keep descending.

It was as if the parable of the Good Samaritan was being re-enacted on a freezing Alaskan mountainside: everyone else passing by on the other side of the road, while one man did the right, neighbourly thing. With his options running out, and light fading fast, Krissak held on to Tamoi's backpack and walked him down the steep traverse. The other man fell several times, taking Krissak with him, but the Slovak was able to arrest each fall before they slid over the abyss.

They did not get to the camp until after midnight. Krissak called for help on his radio and reinforcements finally arrived. Tamoi was badly dehydrated and had to be given fluids. He was put in a sleeping bag, but spent half the night vomiting. When his condition stabilised, a Korean team took him down to the ranger camp, at 14,200 feet, from where he was able to descend the rest of the mountain on his own. But by the time he got to the bottom, he had no memory of being rescued or of being helped down the mountain by Krissak. He had had such a close brush with death that he had become delirious.

Krissak, for his part, refused to cast himself as a hero. Questioned about the incident by an Alaskan National Park Service ranger, he admitted that he had developed frostbite in his feet during the rescue, and his feet were still causing pain, but felt he had done 'nothing out of the ordinary'.

The ranger begged to disagree. On his recommendation, Krissak was named Denali Pro Mountaineer of the Year for 1999, an annual award for climbers in Alaska who go to the assistance of other climbers in trouble. Few previous recipients can have done so much to earn it.

How can one explain what happened on Mount McKinley? All those other climbers – eleven of them – acting selfishly, callously, without any apparent regard for human life. And a twelfth man, alone, unaided, following a quite different script, and doing the decent, honourable thing. Are the good guys in life that outnumbered? The moral of the story is terrifying if you ponder it too deeply.

Perhaps, without having been there, one should not pass judgement on those nameless others who refused to help Tamoi. Perhaps one should look at the story in a different way, ignore the villains and concentrate on the hero. Who was Michal Krissak? And what made him special?

The answer to the riddle – some of it, at any rate – is touchingly simple.

Milan Krissak, his father, was a distinguished mountaineer himself. In 1975, he was part of a Slovakian team that scaled Makalu in the Himalayas, one of the highest, toughest mountains in the world. On the descent, he lost one of his friends and colleagues. He knew what a dangerous business climbing could be. He was no stranger to tragedy.

When not climbing himself, Milan Krissak served with Horska Suzba, a mountain rescue service in the Tatra mountains, between Slovakia and Poland. In 1979, he was in a helicopter flying to the aid of climbers in distress when the helicopter hit a mountain and exploded, killing all on board.

Michal Krissak – the son he left behind, the future hero of Mount McKinley – was just a year old.

He may have grown up without a father. He also grew up with an innate understanding of the unwritten laws of mountaineering.

Eusebio: Portuguese Man of Peace

In one of the most famous of cricket poems, Francis Thompson harks back to a match he saw in his youth:

> For the field is full of shades as I near the shadowy
>   coast,
> And a ghostly batsman plays to the bowling of a
>   ghost,
> And I look through my tears on a soundless-clapping
>   host
> As the run-stealers flicker to and fro,
> To and fro:-
> O my Hornby and my Barlow long ago!

Paradoxically, the batsmen being described – Hornby and Barlow were a pair of cricketing journeymen who opened the batting for Lancashire in the 1880s – are at once indistinct, a blur, and indelibly three-dimensional. In the collective memory of cricket lovers, they have been flickering to and fro ever since.

For sports fans of my generation, born in the 1950s, there is something similarly iconic – a fugitive, flickering beauty – about the sporting heroes we first saw on black-and-white television. They belong to a very specific historical era, which was brief in duration and, once past, could never return. At the start of the 1960s, very few of us had televisions at all; by the time of the 1970 World Cup in Mexico we could watch the action in colour. It was progress. Of course it was progress. But something intangible had been lost.

If you watch, say, a tape of Gary Sobers hitting six sixes in an over against Glamorgan in 1968, what is fascinating is how fuzzy everything looks. The television technology of the day produced images that, even compared to the Hollywood classics of the black-and-white era, seem fragile and ephemeral. How long before they have to be digitally remastered before we can enjoy them at all? But in their very fragility lies their beauty. You watch them with a sense of privilege that the sporting heroes of the past can still weave their magic.

Of course, the great sporting event of the black-and-white era – Germans, look away now – was the 1966 World Cup Final at Wembley. But it was very nearly upstaged by the 1968 European Cup Final in the same stadium, the most glorious night in Manchester United's history. George Best dancing past Benfica defenders. Bobby Charlton lifting the trophy. Matt Busby wiping away tears. The ghosts of Munich hovering in the background. Indelible images.

And right at the heart of it – indistinct, imperishable – a sublime moment of sportsmanship from the great Benfica forward Eusebio.

We all knew Eusebio. If we were English, we all feared Eusebio. Two years before, when England faced Portugal in the semi-final of the World Cup, it was the genius of Eusebio that represented the biggest potential stumbling block. After Pele, he was probably the most brilliant striker in the world. Matches played: 715. Goals scored: 727. His career stats speak for themselves.

And, already, because of 1966, we knew him as a great sportsman. After England had beaten Portugal 2-1, Eusebio was in floods of tears as he departed down the Wembley tunnel. But before that – in a moment that produced one of the great sporting photographs – he had sought out Bobby Charlton, scorer of the two England goals, to congratulate him, patting the Englishman's cheeks in appreciation. Look at the photograph and it is impossible, as it should be, to tell which of the players had finished on the winning side.

Eusebio could, should, have won the European Cup for Benfica at Wembley. With less than ten minutes to go, and the score tied at 1-1, he was put through on goal and had only Alex Stepney to beat. If he had steered the ball – and how easy football is when you have Harry Hindsight in your team – he would surely have scored. Instead he tried to blast it, score a show-stopping, net-busting goal that would break Manchester United hearts. Wrong choice. His shot was ferociously struck, but too close to the goalkeeper, and a grateful Alex Stepney clung on to it.

There have been better saves in big matches, hundreds of them – Stepney hardly had to move – but there has never been a better reaction to a save. As the United goalkeeper made to throw the ball to a colleague, Eusebio, following through, patted him on the back. It was a wonderful gesture.

And Eusebio wasn't done. Play resumed, Stepney threw the ball upfield and, instead of tracking back to defend, the Portuguese forward stood there applauding him. Who *was* this man? He had done his bit. He had shown his appreciation. He had patted Stepney on the back. And now, just in case that was not a generous enough gesture, he was clapping. This was serial gallantry, repetitive chivalry syndrome, the sporting equivalent of a VC and bar.

Kenneth Wolstenholme, commentating, was as star-struck as anyone, including me watching bug-eyed in a village in Surrey. 'What a sportsman, Eusebio! When he could have won the match, to applaud Stepney like that!'

'At the time, I didn't really take it in, to be honest,' Stepney remembers. 'He struck his shot sweetly, but it was more or less straight at me. After I had clung on to it, my first thought was to throw the ball to Tony Dunne, so we could start an attack ourselves – there were only a few minutes of normal time left. But when I watched the replay later, its significance sunk in. I don't ever remember a forward congratulating me on making a save, not like that, not while play was still going on.'

Nowadays, as I joked earlier in the book, when the English visit Portugal, the baggage of cultural prejudice which they carry with them has been shaped – none too flatteringly – by Cristiano Ronaldo and José Mourinho, conceited men in a graceless age.

In 1968, a Portuguese footballer with very different values – so different that they seem to belong to the pre-television age, never mind the era of black-and-white television – made himself an icon of sporting gallantry.

For a few sweet seconds I was in love with him, the way, forty years later, I would be in love with Freddie Flintoff. Score lines fade in the memory. The most brilliant goals dim with time. But great acts of sportsmanship – and this was one of the greatest of them all — make an impression that never leaves you.

Gustavo Kuerten: Brazilian Man of Mystery

If Eusebio's sportsmanship at Wembley was seen and admired by millions, how many viewers in this country saw Brazilian tennis star Gustavo Kuerten show equal gallantry during a match in the States in the late 1990s? A few thousand? Maybe not even that.

The match was screened late in the evening, on a satellite channel, and I have no idea what I was doing watching it – my tennis watching rarely extends beyond Wimbledon. Perhaps it was half-time at Stamford Bridge or rain had stopped play in Barbados. Compulsive channel hopping is the lot of the sporting couch potato. We are a sad, solitary breed, and I often raise a silent glass to those others – in Solihull, in Manchester, in Chipping Norton – who have serendipitously ended up on the same channel as me, glued to strange sports played in strange countries, thousands of miles away. Only one thing lures us in, and only one thing keeps us hooked – we don't know what's going to happen next.

We could certainly never have anticipated the script on this occasion. Gustavo 'Guga' Kuerten was still a relative newcomer on the international scene. He had won his first French Open when he was just twenty and, with his film-star looks and unkempt hair, exuded a certain chaotic Latin-American charm. There was something about him: the enthusiasm of a boy; the flamboyance of a showman; the playfulness of a clown. Perhaps that is why, having strayed on to a tennis channel, I lingered there. The score was 5-5 in a tie-break, so I thought, I'll just see out the set, then go to bed.

Biff-bang, biff-bang, biff-bang. The rallies ebbed and flowed, with Kuerten, as was his wont, grunting theatrically after every shot. 5-5 became 6-6 became 7-7. It was excellent stuff – although, of course, from my point of view, not quite cricket. Where were the nuances, the tactical subtleties? I stifled a yawn and looked at my watch. Would I even bother to see out the set?

And then, like a flash of lightning, it happened. At 9-9, a long rally ended with Kuerten's opponent passing him with a running forehand. Set point! Except that none of us – not me in Oxford, not Jim in Solihull, not Dave in Manchester, not Barry in Chipping Norton – was looking at the scoreboard. We were looking open-mouthed at Kuerten.

Left flat-footed by the passing shot, the Brazilian dropped his racquet, bowed in acknowledgement then, incredibly, ran right across the court, and around the side of the net, to shake his opponent by the hand.

I had never seen anything like it. It was like watching the ghost of Eusebio at Wembley, a throwback to the golden age of chivalry. And to think that, but for my compulsive channel hopping, my addiction to the thrills and spills of televised sport, I would have been tucked up in bed with a good book! At such moments, the life of a couch potato ceases to be sad: it becomes transcendent.

Who was this man? He was a professional tennis player. He was playing in a big tournament. He was locked in a nerve-jangling tie-break. He was about to have to serve to stay in the set. By rights, by the dreary mantras of his profession, he should have had only one thought in his head: *Concentrate. Stay in the zone. Don't think about the last point. Think about the next point.* But the emotions of the moment – an appreciation of his opponent's brilliance and an impulse to show that appreciation – were just too much for him. He ran around the net, like an untrained puppy, because he couldn't help himself.

How could I go to bed while I was still mesmerised by this new sporting hero? I sat up late, watched Kuerten lose the tie-break, watched him lose the match, watched him congratulate his opponent at the net with the same puppy-like generosity. I was enchanted. I couldn't get enough of the man.

In the morning, still under his spell, I Googled him. I was expecting to read about a child prodigy, a playboy going through life with a carefree smile. I could hardly have been more wrong. Kuerten lost his father when he was just eight years old. He gave all his trophies to his younger brother, who was severely disabled. He wasn't generous-natured because he was young at heart: he was generous-natured because he had grown up too fast. He knew, better than most players, how trivial it was to win a tennis match.

And he had expressed that maturity of outlook in the most vivid, captivating way.

*

Or had I dreamed the whole thing?

When I started writing this book, and was looking back on great moments of sportsmanship I had been lucky enough to witness, Gustavo Kuerten was one of the first names on my team sheet. All I had to do was look up the match and find out who his opponent was.

Disaster! How does one look up a tennis match? If Kuerten had been a cricketer, I would simply have consulted *Wisden*, the holy of holies. The research would have taken a matter of minutes. Not only would all the scores from all his matches have been faithfully recorded, but also any episodes of exceptional interest, of which this was clearly one. *Net, player running around for purposes of congratulating opponent.* The trusty *Wisden* index would have led me straight to my quarry.

Tennis is less lovingly chronicled. There are umpteen places where one can look up career stats, service stats, tie-break stats, all the stuff the tennis anoraks need to keep them happy. But there is not the same relish for tales of the unexpected – pigeons stopping play, commentators getting sunstroke, identical twins featuring in the same match – as there is in cricket.

All the bookshops in Oxford could not help me discover when and against whom Kuerten had been playing when he had so thrilled me ten years before. I looked up his Wikipedia entry, expecting to find something there. Nothing. I entered 'Kuerten' and 'sportsmanship' into search engines and scrolled through page after page. Still nothing. I consulted tennis-mad friends, the sort who queue all night to get Centre Court seats at Wimbledon. Hopeless.

The possibility had to be faced that I had simply imagined the whole thing. Or that it had been a totally different player. Not Brazilian, Colombian. Not called Kuerten, called Merryman.

And then I remembered Jim, Dave and Barry – those unseen others, my fellow couch potatoes, watching the same match on television on the same day, as spellbound as me by what they had seen. For how could they not be spellbound? It was a magical moment in sport.

Feeling vaguely sheepish, as if I was accessing a hard-core porn site, I found a tennis forum on the internet and joined it under the user name 'Corinthian'. I was asked my real name, gave it, asked my age, gave it, asked my country of residence, gave it, asked why I was interested in joining the forum, lied ('Because I'm tennis-mad and love chatting to like-minded people in other countries') and, after a short hiatus, while I was vetted by the forum administrator, was finally admitted to the freemasonry of tennis.

Fingers trembling in anticipation, I found the page headed 'How to Start a New Thread' and began typing. 'Sportsmanship. Can anybody help me? I am sure I remember Gustavo Kuerten, in a match in the late nineties . . .' Then I logged off and popped out for a curry. As I left the house, my eye was caught by the 2006 *Wisden* on the bookshelf and I gave a rueful grimace. Things are so simple in cricket.

When I got back, a couple of hours later, and rejoined the forum, I could hardly believe my eyes. There were already eight responses to my question, from all over the world. Not all of them were relevant. One was a shaggy dog story about Tiger Woods and Roger Federer in a helicopter. One looked suspiciously like a gay chat-up line. But one of them, indubitably, was right on the money.

It was from 'Burrow' in Turkey (*Burrow?* Who was this guy? Roger Rabbit from Istanbul?) and read: 'For sure Kuerten did that. Was in 1999 US Open quarter-final against Pioline.'

Gotcha. Now that I had got the year, the tournament and the opponent – Frenchman Cedric Pioline – it was the easiest thing in the world to Google a contemporary account of the match.

'Kuerten won the entertainment stakes by acclamation inside the Arthur Ashe stadium,' wrote the *New York Times* reporter. 'The fans chanted his nickname as if they had entered a trance.'

Of the Big Point, the one that had so captivated me, the reporter had this to say: 'When Pioline connected with a spectacular running forehand pass that put him ahead by 10-9 in the third-set tie-breaker, Kuerten dropped his racquet, genuflected and moved over to Pioline's side of the court to pay his respects with a handshake. That's his version of hand-to-hand combat.'

The Brazilian, who was trying to reach his first US Open semi-final, lost three successive tie-breaks, which is always a tough way to lose, but was philosophical in defeat. Questioned about his act of sportsmanship, he simply said: 'It was a great point. Maybe best point in the match. I couldn't believe it. I play well that point, he play better than me, so I congratulate him. Was an amazing shot.'

He play better than me, so I congratulate him. It is the language of a child, the logic of a child. But in sport, as in so much else, children can be wiser than adults. They are not yet blinded by cynicism. They are too young to have acquired tunnel vision. They can see the big picture, bright and clear.

Thanks, Gustavo.

And thanks, Burrow.

Musical Chairs at Wimbledon

It was two of my new buddies in the tennis forum – 'Zolka' from Italy and 'Mrs Fedex' from Vatican City – who put me on to another lovely piece of sportsmanship, this one involving Roger Federer. The incident occurred at Wimbledon in 2008, when Federer was defending champion. Mrs Fedex, bless her, kindly sent me a link to the *Daily Telegraph* sports section.

Federer was playing Dominik Hrbaty of Slovakia in a first-round match on Centre Court, and was about to serve for the third set at 5-2. As he had not faced a break point on his serve all match, the result of the match was pretty much a foregone conclusion, just minutes away – at which point, as the players changed ends, Hrbaty made a decidedly unorthodox suggestion. Would Federer mind if they sat next to each other at the changeover, rather than in their customary seats separated by the umpire's chair?

Of course not, said a surprised Federer, that was no

problem, there was an extra seat – whereupon, to the delight of the crowd, the two men spent the change-over chatting and laughing, rather than in their separate zones, staring grimly into the middle distance. The unwritten conventions of tennis had been blown wide open – the way Gustavo Kuerten had blown them wide open by crossing to his opponent's side of the net.

'Dominik and I go way back,' explained Federer afterwards. 'We used to play doubles together. We used to practise together. We've always had fun together. He said it might be his last Wimbledon, so it was all a bit emotional. It was nice he did that. It was nice to share that moment on Centre Court together.'

As the two men chatted, Hrbaty told Federer it was not just an honour to play against him, but an honour to be his friend. 'Well, same here for me,' said Federer. The courtesies pinged to and fro like well-hit forehands.

It was a touching moment. It showed that the sense of fun had not gone from professional tennis. It produced smiles where one did not expect smiles. Here were two men competing in the biggest tournament in the world, with huge prize money at stake, giving their all with every point – but able, between points, to switch off, relax, remember it was only a game.

One of the enemies of sport – not as obviously sinister as drugs, but just as corrosive – is the dourness of outlook that comes with long years of training and self-discipline. You see it in golfers, you see it in footballers, you see it in most professional sportsmen. They wind themselves up like coiled springs in the changing room, then put on their game faces – one of the sillier sporting clichés – when they go out on the pitch. There is nothing remotely game about those faces: they are the faces of zombies, robots.

Hrbaty and Federer joshing and joking lightened the whole mood. It could never have happened in a more closely contested match, and perhaps one would not have wanted it to happen in a more closely contested match. Gladiators are not clowns. But in context, it was not just appropriate, but heartwarming.

When play resumed and Federer won the first point of the game with a service winner, a man in the crowd shouted, 'Give him a chance, Roger!' Federer was reduced to giggles, which lightened the mood even more. But nobody minded the descent into frivolity. It was a reminder of the good humour, good manners, good fellowship, that lie at the heart of sport.

Lutz Long: The Man Who Defied Hitler

'We were just two uncertain young men in an uncertain world,' said American athlete Jesse Owens of one of the most celebrated friendships in sport. It was a friendship measured in days, even hours, as fugitive in its beauty as a sunset or a daffodil swaying in the breeze. But if ever the noblest ideals of sport put the world beyond sport to shame, this was the moment.

Jesse Owens is a name that still resonates, even among people with no interest in sport. He was the great party-pooper, the man who ensured, virtually single-handedly, that Hitler's attempts to turn the 1936 Berlin Olympics into a Nazi propaganda coup, filmed for posterity by Leni Riefenstahl, would end in ignominy. The Führer could rave all he wanted about Aryan supremacy and the master race. He could say, and did say, 'Americans ought to be ashamed of themselves for letting their medals be worn by Negroes.' But if an African-American athlete could take the gold medals in Berlin, eclipsing those blond German supermen, his ravings would be exposed as just that, ravings.

Seventy years on, the name of Lutz Long has been largely forgotten. Born Carl Ludwig Long in Leipzig in 1913, the German athlete was the walking embodiment of Aryan ideals: blond, blue-eyed, super-fit; a magnificent physical specimen. But in the cold print of sporting records his achievements are too modest to have withstood the erosion of time.

Long was a long-jumper, an unglamorous discipline, and after finishing third in the 1934 European Athletics Championship was fancied to be among the medals again in Berlin. His main rival, it was assumed, would be Owens, who had already won the first of his gold medals in the 100m.

The long-jump event took place on 4 August and, in the preliminary rounds, it was Long who took the lead, setting an Olympic record in the process. Owens, by contrast, was struggling. His first two jumps were fouls and, with only one jump remaining, he was in danger of being eliminated and missing the final round. He cut a disconsolate figure, sitting on the ground looking dejected, his brain scrambled. Defeat beckoned and, like many an athlete in a similar situation, he had trouble thinking straight. He badly needed some hard-headed tactical advice – and he got it, from an unexpected quarter.

His German rival, to his astonishment, came up to him and made a suggestion in broken English, using his towel to demonstrate what he meant. Why didn't Owens simply mark out his run again and, to avoid the risk of foot-fault-ing, take off from a point several inches behind the line? He only needed to clear 7.15m to advance to the next round – comfortably within his abilities – so there was no need, tactically, to attempt anything too ambitious at this stage of the competition.

'You can melt down all the medals and cups I have won,' Owens wrote in his memoirs, 'and they wouldn't be worth the plating on the 24-carat friendship I felt for Lutz Long at that moment.'

Owens duly took the German's advice, re-marked his run and qualified for the final round with something to spare. He went on to take the gold medal, with a jump of 8.08m, consigning Long, with 7.87m, to the silver. The German, in the best Olympic traditions, was the first to congratulate his opponent, and the two men celebrated together before returning arm-in-arm to the dressing-room, cheered by a hundred thousand German fans.

'It took a lot of courage for him to befriend me in front of Hitler,' Owens reflected afterwards. 'Hitler must have gone crazy watching us embrace.' But embrace they did, in the way of athletes through the ages. Sport, the great leveller, the smasher of political barriers, had carried the day.

That night the two men held a faltering conversation in the Olympic village. They discovered that they had more in common than they realised. Both had been born into rural families that had had to move to the city to find work. Both were married with one child. Friendship stretched across the great divide of race and language.

So much has been written about the Berlin Olympics, so much of what happened has passed into the realm of sporting folklore, that it is easy to miss some of the nuances of the Long–Owens story.

There is a myth, for example, that Hitler snubbed Owens

and refused to shake his hand at the medals ceremony. In fact, having originally wanted to shake only German medal winners by the hand, but been told by the Olympic Committee that was unacceptable, Hitler refused to shake any winning athletes by the hand.

'Hitler didn't snub me,' said Owens. 'When I passed him, he waved his hand at me, and I waved back. It was FDR who snubbed me. The President didn't even send me a telegram.'

It was not only in Germany, in other words, that notions of Aryan supremacy held sway in the 1930s. One of the great ironies of the Berlin Olympics is that Owens, after sailing the Atlantic third-class, was allowed to stay in the same hotels as white athletes, in a way unimaginable in America at the time. When he returned to the States, he got a ticker-tape welcome in New York, then had to take the freight elevator to the reception in his honour at the Waldorf-Astoria Hotel. FDR snubbed him. So did Harry Truman. It was not until Eisenhower was President that Owens was finally invited to the White House.

His post-Berlin career was inglorious, even humiliating. To make ends meet, the finest athlete of his generation was reduced to racing against horses and dogs in novelty events. 'People said it was degrading for an Olympic champion to run against a horse,' remembered Owens. 'But what was I supposed to do? I had four gold medals, but you can't eat gold medals.'

Lutz Long suffered an even grimmer fate, dying of his wounds in an Allied hospital in Sicily in 1943. The two friends never saw each other after the Berlin Olympics, although Owens did establish contact with Long's family after the war.

But their brief, intense friendship, not the medals they

won, is their memorial. Somehow its brevity only empha-
sises its sweetness, the fact that it happened naturally,
casually, like the smile of two strangers passing in the street.
All that they had in common was that they were athletes,
members of the same human race. But that was enough.

Friendships which span racial divides are so common in
modern sport that we take them for granted. But it was not
always so. Until comparatively recently, within the memory
of many sports fans, a white sportsman extending the hand
of friendship to a black one, or vice versa, was making a
statement of huge symbolic significance. Throughout sporting history there have been moments when sport has not
simply mirrored social change, but anticipated social change.
A fine example of that is provided by the Australian rules
footballer Haydn Bunton who, in the narrow-minded
Melbourne of the 1930s, went out of his way to befriend an
Aboriginal team-mate – in a way unimaginable in the world
beyond sport.

Lutz Long befriending Jesse Owens was revolutionary in
the same way, nudging consciences, challenging the accepted
social order. There is an old photograph of the two men on
the podium during the medals ceremony. Owens is saluting
the Stars and Stripes. Long is giving a Nazi salute. They
could be inhabitants of different planets. Politically, they
were. But in the alchemy of sport those differences had dis-
solved into nothingness.

Gottfried von Cramm: The Gay Baron of Tennis

Lutz Long was not the only German sportsman to run the gauntlet of Hitler's disapproval.

Baron Gottfried Alexander Maximilian Walter Kurt von Cramm was one of the most colourful tennis players of the inter-war period. He was one of seven sons of a Hanover nobleman who had introduced him to the game on the family estate. Handsome, wealthy and a dashing stylist, von Cramm had a small physical flaw worthy of a James Bond villain – he had lost the top joint of his right index finger while feeding sugar lumps to a horse.

Von Cramm never won Wimbledon, having to be content with three runner-up spots, but played a prominent part in the German Davis Cup team in the 1930s, when tennis was becoming increasingly embroiled in politics. In 1933, Daniel Prenn, a player of Polish-Jewish origins, was kicked off the German team at the insistence of the Nazi regime. Von Cramm was openly critical of the decision and, despite repeated invitations by Goering to join the Nazi Party, refused to do so. The seeds of his own downfall had been sown.

Two years later, in 1935, Germany found itself pitched against the United States in a Davis Cup tie at Wimbledon. Von Cramm and his doubles partner, Kay Lund, were involved in an epic five-set match against the American pairing of Wilmer Allison and John van Ryn. The match was fiercely contested and pivoted on a remarkable moment of sportsmanship in the deciding set.

The Germans had five match points, one of which they seemed to have converted when von Cramm and Lund both went for the same ball and Lund returned it for a winner. 'Game, set and match to Germany,' announced the umpire. But the baron was having none of it. He immediately gestured that the ball had tipped his racquet on the way through to his partner. The point was awarded to the Americans, who went on to win the match and the tie.

In the locker-room afterwards, von Cramm was rounded on by his team-mates and accused of letting down his country. The baron was outraged. 'Let me get something straight right now,' he reportedly said. 'When I chose tennis as a young man, I chose it because it was a gentleman's game, and that is the way I've always played it. Do you think I could sleep tonight knowing that the ball had touched my racquet without my saying so? Never! I don't think I'm letting the German people down. I think I'm doing them credit.'

Von Cramm's actions remained a source of controversy in Germany, although he was far too important to the Davis Cup team to be sacked. In 1937, again at Wimbledon, his

brilliance took Germany to the brink of what would have
been its first ever Davis Cup. Everything hinged on the final
singles match between von Cramm and the great American
Don Budge. The game was played on a packed Centre
Court in front of a crowd which included Queen Mary and
the German Ambassador to Great Britain, Joachim von
Ribbentrop.

For von Cramm, given his prickly relations with the
Nazis, the stakes could scarcely have been higher. Shortly
before the match, he was called to the telephone to take a
long-distance call. It was the Führer, wishing him luck. No
pressure then. With the swastika flying over the court, and
his heart pounding, the baron strode out to meet his destiny.
The match turned out to be a classic, one of the most celebrated in the history of the Davis Cup.

'The suspense was almost unbearable,' wrote Allison
Danzig of the *New York Times*. 'Shots that would have stood
out vividly in the average match were commonplace in the
cascade of electrifying strokes that stemmed from the rac-
quets of two superb fighters . . . At last it was over, and von
Cramm, with the fine sportsmanship which won his every
rival to him, came forward with a sunny smile to shake the
hand of his opponent. He had lost the most important
match of his life, but took his defeat as nobly as he had
played.'

Sadly for von Cramm, it was not the kind of nobility
that Hitler appreciated. The following year, after the baron
had publicly criticised the Nazis during a visit to Australia,
he was arrested by the Gestapo at his family castle and
charged with 'sexual irregularities', namely having had a
homosexual affair with a Jewish actor called Manasse
Herbst. Von Cramm was convicted in private and sentenced
to a year in prison. The allegations were almost certainly

true. But would charges have been brought if von Cramm had won his match against Budge? Or if he hadn't been too honest for his own good in the earlier match? Wouldn't his status as a national sporting hero, the man who brought the Davis Cup home to Germany, have made him unassailable?

In a story of many strands, it is impossible not to warm to the man at the heart of it: born in the wrong country, at the wrong time, antagonising the wrong people; having sex with the wrong people; yet, on the tennis court, burning with an almost messianic sense of the right way to play the game.

Gottfried von Cramm's war was almost as dramatic as his exploits in the Davis Cup. On his release from prison, still out of favour with the Nazis, he was sent to the Russian front as a private. The intention was to humiliate him: the baron had been a reserve officer in the Germany army. But he was not found wanting on the battlefield. At Stalingrad, despite frostbite in both legs, he held off Soviet troops with a machine gun long enough to enable his men to effect a daring escape. The action earned him the Iron Cross. Later, in yet another twist, he was dishonourably discharged from the army, on suspicion of plotting against Hitler. He was a great patriot, but he could never, ever be a Nazi.

Few sporting lives, in any sport, have been quite so governed by principle. German aristocrats are proverbially stiff and inflexible. Gottfried von Cramm retained the inflexibility, but added a delightful dimension of grace.

Max Schmeling: 'I'm Almost Glad I Lost that Fight'

To the names of Lutz Long and Gottfried von Cramm there can be added a third great German sportsman of the 1930s who refused to toe the Nazi line – Max Schmeling, the only one of his countrymen to be crowned world heavyweight boxing champion.

He won the title in New York in 1930, much against the odds, when his American opponent, Jack Sharkey, was disqualified for punching below the belt; he then relinquished it two years later, to the same opponent, on a disputed decision. 'We wuz robbed!' complained his manager, in what would become a sporting catchphrase. But those fights, dramatic though they were, form only a small part of the Max Schmeling story.

The great German champion died in 2005, at the age of ninety-nine. If he had made it to a century he would have joined a very exclusive club indeed – practically a one-man club in the harsh world of boxing. Born under the Kaiser, and christened Maximillian Adolf Otto Siegfried, he lived to see his country lose two world wars, be carved into two, reunited, practically bankrupt itself, recover, host two Olympics and win three football World Cups.

Paradoxically, despite his longevity, his fifteen minutes of sporting celebrity, when the eyes of the world were upon him, lasted just two minutes and four seconds – which is as long as it took Joe Louis to knock him out in their cele-brated title fight at the Yankee Stadium on 22 June 1938.

If the Berlin Olympics had a political/racial subtext, by 1938 the subtext had become a banner headline. America versus Germany. Democracy versus tyranny. The Brown Bomber versus the Aryan superman. As the world lurched towards war, those two men in boxing shorts carried so much symbolic baggage, had so much invested in them, were the repository of so many hopes, the conduits of so much hatred, that it is a wonder they got into the ring at all.

To top it all, Schmeling and Louis had what sports com-mentators call 'history'. In 1936, in one of the biggest upsets in boxing, the German had achieved a twelfth-round knock-out against Louis, who had never previously been stopped and had seemed unbeatable. At the Yankee Stadium the American was out for revenge, retribution – and set about it with rare ferocity.

Feelings were running dangerously high. Before the fight, Roosevelt invited Louis to the White House for a patriotic pep talk. 'Joe,' he said, 'we need muscles like yours to beat Germany.' A Nazi publicist countered by promising that Schmeling would win, and that his prize money would be used to build German tanks. Anti-Nazi protesters picketed the hotel where the German was staying. There was sulphur in the air.

In the ring, perhaps mercifully, proceedings were nasty, brutish and short. Louis had his opponent on the canvas four times before the German was counted out. It was a rout, a humiliation. Sportsmanship never got a look-in. There was no feel-good moment, no chivalrous embrace between winner and loser. While Louis gloated, Schmeling cried foul, claiming he had been felled by an illegal kidney punch. To the New York fans, and the American media, it was a narrative of cartoon-like simplicity: the bad guy from the bad country had been given a well-deserved thrashing.

How little they knew the real Max Schmeling. He may have been used as a propaganda tool by the Nazis, but he was no more a Nazi than the fans were. He was courted by Hitler and Goebbels, but persistently refused to join the Party. When put under pressure to fire his Jewish-American manager, Joe Jacobs, he was similarly disobliging.

Of his humiliation at the Yankee Stadium, Schmeling said in an interview in 1975: 'I'm almost glad I lost that fight. Just imagine if I would have come back to Germany with a victory. I had nothing to do with the Nazis, but they would have given me a medal. After the war, I might have been considered a war criminal.'

The German might have been beaten in the ring, but a few months after the fight he showed the sort of stuff he was made of. During the infamous Kristallnacht in November 1938, when synagogues were burning all over Berlin, the boxer hid two teenage sons of a Jewish friend in his hotel room. Later, at great risk to himself, he helped smuggle the two boys out of Germany. Like Gottfried von Cramm, he fought for his country, serving in the Luftwaffe, but not as a Nazi.

After the war he was briefly interned by the Allies, then had to carry on boxing for a time, despite being over forty, to make ends meet. His circumstances only improved when a former New York boxing commissioner who had become a Coca-Cola executive offered him a share of the German franchise in the company. This enabled the boxer to pursue a successful business career and, later, become a well-known philanthropist.

The man who had humiliated him at the Yankee Stadium was not so lucky. Joe Louis became a poster hero during the war, promising 'We're gonna win 'cause we're on God's side', but afterwards was dogged by financial problems. He carried on boxing far too long and, for a time, was reduced to earning money as a professional wrestler. But, as memories of war receded, there was to be a touching rapprochement between the former adversaries. The good sportsmanship that had been lacking in 1938 finally blossomed.

Schmeling and Louis met up again in 1954, after an episode of *This Is Your Life*, and became firm friends, meeting on at least a dozen further occasions. The German discreetly helped the American settle his medical bills and, in 1981, according to some accounts, helped pay for his funeral, at which he was a pallbearer. It was an unlikely, touching relationship, celebrated in the 2002 movie, *Joe and Max*.

The young men who had been used as political pawns found their destinies intertwined by a different imperative – reconciliation.

Gary Sobers: Doing Good by Stealth

Modesty, as we have seen, goes hand in hand in chivalry. To act generously, then expect to be patted on the back for it, devalues the act. You will never hear the true sportsman boasting of his exploits. He would rather his good deeds passed without comment – or, better still, went completely unnoticed.

In his biography of Gary Sobers, the great West Indian cricketer, Trevor Bailey tells a charming story illustrating this point. On the field, Sobers was one of the most gifted players in the history of the game, someone who could win a match single-handed with a brilliant innings or inspired spell of bowling. Off the field, he was modesty personified, winning friends the world over with his shy, gap-toothed smile. There was no trace of the arrogance that so often accompanies greatness. He played the game for fun.

The first time I saw Gary Sobers bat, in a Test match at Edgbaston, I could hear him laughing – he was sharing a joke with an England fielder – from my seat on the boundary's edge, nearly a hundred yards away. To my earnest schoolboy mind, sportsmen were not meant to laugh, or not during the serious business of trying to win a Test for their country. That little eruption of mirth, carried to me on the wind, was so deliciously unexpected that it felt like an epiphany: an object lesson in how cricket should be played. Small wonder that he became one of my great sporting idols.

In the pub after the game, or when rain has stopped play, cricketers will spend literally hours, *Wisden* in hand, debating which was the greatest of all cricket teams. Bradman's 1948 Invincibles? The West Indies battering ram of the early 1980s? Or the all-conquering Aussies of the Waugh–Ponting era? There are some strong contenders and the race is too close to call. But change the terms of reference slightly, and ask which was the most loved of all cricket teams, and there is a runaway winner: Frank Worrell's never-to-be-forgotten West Indies side of the early 1960s, which captivated fans all around the world.

It was the joy with which they played the game – the same exuberance of expression one associates with Brazilian footballers – that lingers in the memory. Whether it was Wes Hall loping in to bowl, Lance Gibbs with his puckish off-breaks or Rohan Kanhai attempting extravagant sweep shots, the body language carried the same message: we're playing cricket because it's fun. And at the heart of that joy was Gary Sobers, the laughing cavalier.

In the story Bailey tells about Sobers he is not laughing but using his cunning, like the Artful Dodger in reverse: not taking by stealth, but giving by stealth.

'It is easy to give one's wicket away,' Bailey writes, 'but it takes an artist to do it as well as Gary did to me in a bene-fit match in the 1960s. He decided he had provided sufficient entertainment and had scored enough runs, so he got out. Nothing unusual about that. It was the way he did it which typified both the man and his craft. He waited until I sent down a ball of good length which pitched on his leg stump and hit the middle as he played a forward defen-sive stroke, deliberately and fractionally down the wrong line. He made it look a very good delivery – it wasn't a bad one. But he played his shot so well that the wicket-keeper and first slip – though both county professionals – came up to congratulate me. I knew instinctively what Gary had done. But no spectator realised it was an act of charity; only Gary and myself.'

What a strange, touching story! It is as if the giver and the recipient of the gift are part of a secret conspiracy, thrilling to the fact that they know something nobody else knows. If Sobers had ostentatiously hit a catch up in the air, or aimed a wild slog at a straight ball, it would have been an empty gesture, giving no real pleasure to anyone. His clever sub-terfuge, winning Bailey slaps on the back from his team-mates, revealed a deeper, more mischievous imagina-tion. It brought a hint of Christmas to the summer game – for isn't the beauty of the Santa Claus myth the fact that the present-giver is too modest to reveal himself, but slinks off into the night while the children sleep?

Sobers the cricketer had to endure the media spotlight to which his genius exposed him. The first batsman to hit six sixes in an over was the object of awe wherever cricket was played. Sobers the man just wanted the quiet life; he bridled at applause, celebrity, the adulation of strangers. To make a sporting gesture, but on the sly, disdaining the fruits of his sportsmanship, was wholly typical of a gentle, self-effacing man.

I was reminded of the Trevor Bailey story years later when – joy unconfined – I got to play against Gary Sobers in a match at the Hurlingham Club in London. He was in his mid-fifties, but still a consummate batsman, stroking the ball effortlessly to all parts of the field. His timing was so immaculate that it came as a complete surprise when he got himself out – clean bowled by Graham Allen, the Labour MP for Nottingham North. He played a studious-looking defensive stroke, but *down the wrong line*. We all whooped with delight and mobbed the bowler. It seemed providential somehow: the great man humbled by an MP from Nottinghamshire, the county Sobers had once represented.

Or perhaps too providential?

Graham is a lovely man, far too nice to be a politician, and has doubtless been dining off this story – and who wouldn't? – ever since. Arthur Conan Doyle once got W. G. Grace out and was so chuffed that he wrote a long poem to celebrate the occasion. These fantasies made flesh are the quintessence of sport.

I can see Graham propping up a bar in Nottingham, regaling his constituents with the story of the wickedly swerving off-cutter with which he pierced the great man's forward defence. Perhaps he even re-enacts the incident, with a pork pie as the ball and a bar stool as the wicket. If he has grandchildren, they will have heard the story a thousand times. No speech he has made in the House of Commons will have given him such intense pleasure.

And Gary Sobers being Gary Sobers – as modest a genius as ever played the game – nobody will ever know how good a ball it really was.

Fearless Freddie: Taking the Rough with the Smooth

FRANK CORNFIELD

All great men have their Achilles heel and, with Gary Sobers, as has been well documented, it was gambling. His famously generous declaration at Port of Spain in 1968, when he set England a victory target of 215 in 165 minutes, which they knocked off with embarrassing ease, was from the kamikaze school of captaincy: better than a dull draw but, odds-wise, a wild miscalculation. His judgement of horses, notoriously, has been little better.

But gambling, for good or ill, is part and parcel of sport. At its worst, in those grubby match-fixing scandals, it has been a cancer, gnawing at the very heart of sport; at its best, adding colour, pumping up excitement, spawning glorious tales of the unexpected, it has mirrored the ups and downs of the sporting life. The gambler and the sportsman are two sides of the same coin.

When I started writing this book I never imagined that it would feature a bookmaker – a *bookmaker*, for heaven's sake, one of those ferret-faced men in raincoats with satchels of dirty fivers under their arms – as a model of good sportsmanship. But the obituaries of 'Fearless Freddie' Williams, who died in June 2008, forced a rethink. What captivated race-goers about Williams, wrote one obituarist, was the 'Corinthian spirit' with which he plied his trade.

The phrase did not feel like a hyperbole. It perfectly reflected the mind-set of a courteous, phlegmatic man who might have had those famous lines from Kipling engraved above his pitch. 'If you can look on triumph and disaster / And treat those two impostors just the same . . .'

In one sense Williams was an old-fashioned gentleman amateur. He was independently wealthy. He owned a successful bottling business in Scotland. He didn't need the money of which he relieved punters – and of which they, occasionally, relieved him. But that fact alone doesn't explain the popularity he enjoyed in an unpopular profession. There was something about the man. An attitude. A philosophy of life. A smile when others might not have smiled.

The son of a Scottish miner, who walked with a limp after contracting polio as a child, Williams was famous for taking the sort of huge wagers the high street chains wouldn't touch. His high-stakes jousts with the Irish millionaire J. P. McManus were part of racing folklore. At their very first encounter, at Cheltenham in 1999, the Irishman put a whopping £90,000 on a 2-1 favourite, almost as if testing the other man's mettle. Williams accepted the bet without flinching. The horse was leading over the last, but then faded into second place. Round One to Fearless Freddie.

Williams was not always so lucky but, win or lose, he remained a model of equanimity. It was the sport he enjoyed, not the pocketing of huge sums of money. He was as happy taking £2 bets at a Glasgow dog track as mingling with the high-rollers at Cheltenham.

'I get a real buzz from the betting ring,' he once said. 'There is a constant challenge. The reward is not always important. Running a betting shop is just like selling Mars Bars. People come in and give you money. Cheers. The only decision you make is whether to open the door in the morning.'

Wherever Williams went, he made friends with his ebullience and good humour. The worst day of his life, by one of those little sporting quirks, was, at another level, the best day of his life, the one that revealed the greatness of the man, his munificence both of purse and spirit.

He had taken an absolute flogging from McManus at the 2006 Cheltenham Festival, losing £600,000 on a 6-1 shot, then over £300,000 on a 50-1 outsider. He was nearly a million pounds down by the end of the day, and was driving home with his daughter, licking his wounds, when his car was ambushed by an armed gang, who smashed the windscreen with crowbars, helped themselves to his money, then made their getaway, burning their own vehicles to escape detection.

Williams and his daughter, though unhurt, were badly shaken by the incident. But it was not too long before Fearless Freddie was seeing the funny side of the situation. Suppose he had just won £1 million, rather than lost it?

Asked by the police how much money the robbers had taken, he joked: 'Put it this way, after burning out a total of four getaway vehicles, they might have been out of pocket.' His losses were later estimated at £70,000.

Reflecting later on his miserable day, he was typically philosophical: 'I'm always the same, up or down, it makes no difference. You have to be able to take the rough with the smooth, or you wouldn't have any friends or family.'

Two days later, he was back at his pitch at Ayr, where he got a standing ovation from race-goers. They never minded Fearless Freddie relieving them of a few quid: they knew a true sportsman when they saw one.

Eugenio Monti: 'Get an Englishman and a Spanner'

Few sporting lives ended as poignantly as that of Eugenio Monti, the *Rosso Volante*, or, in English, the Flying Redhead. In old age, the great Italian bobsledder contracted Parkinson's disease and, in December 2003, died of self-inflicted gunshot wounds. But long before that his name had become synonymous with good sportsmanship and the Olympic ideal of fair competition.

Born in Dobbiaco in 1928, Monti was a skiing champion in his youth, but had to shift disciplines to the bobsleigh after damaging knee ligaments. He acquired his nickname partly because of his red hair, partly because of the uninhibited, even reckless, way he competed. He got the same sort of buzz out of raw speed as a Formula One racing driver.

Monti quickly rose to the top of his new sport and won his first World Championships in St Moritz in 1957. But

Olympic gold was proving far more elusive. In the 1956 Winter Olympics, in Cortina d'Ampezzo, Monti won silver in both the two-man and four-man sleigh. He was hoping to go one better in 1960, when the Olympics were held in Squaw Valley, California; but to his frustration, for economic reasons the bobsleigh event was not staged.

Would his luck turn in 1964, when the Games were held in Innsbruck in Austria? Logic said yes. Monti was the reigning world champion, the undisputed king of his discipline. But when did sport obey logic? After his earlier disappointments, Monti must have been wondering if, when it came to the Olympics, he was destined to be one of the nearly men of sport, haunted by long-held dreams that proved ultimately unattainable.

It is important to remember those dreams, deep-burning, kept alight by long hours of training. They are the invisible face of sport, the bits the spectators never see. They provide the context for what happened next: not one, but two, conspicuous acts of gallantry.

In the four-man event, the Canadian team of Vic Emery, rank outsiders, had taken the lead when they damaged the axle of their sled, which would have forced them to withdraw. Imagine Emery's astonishment when he found his sled upside down and being torn apart by Monti's mechanics, who were desperately trying to fix it. They sorted the problem, and the Canadians went on to take gold, with the Italians having to be satisfied with bronze.

The two-man event was even more dramatic and featured the up-and-coming British duo of Tony Nash and Robin Dixon. They achieved the fastest time in their first run but, like the Canadians, suffered a mechanical failure. A bolt attaching the runners to the shell had sheared, making the sleigh inoperable. The Flying Redhead, again, stepped into the breach. As he was about to steer his own sleigh down the track, he called out: 'Get an Englishman and a spanner to the finish and they can have my bolt.' Sure enough, as soon as he had finished his own run, the bolt was ferried back to the start and, in the nick of time, attached to the British sleigh.

The result was now a foregone conclusion. Gold for Nash and Dixon. *More* Olympic heartbreak for Monti, who had to settle for bronze.

The Italian press slaughtered him, but the Flying Redhead was unrepentant. 'Nash didn't win because I gave him the bolt,' he said. 'He won because he had the fastest run.'

Others took a less partisan view. The International Olympic Committee was so impressed by what Monti had done that they gave him the inaugural Pierre de Coubertin Medal, named after the founder of the Olympic movement. The medal is awarded to athletes who display outstanding sportsmanship, epitomising the spirit of the Olympics. In nearly half a century there have only been ten recipients of the medal, making it rarer – and, depending on your view of these things, more prestigious – than Olympic gold.

At times, the Pierre de Coubertin Medal can seem like a consolation prize, as dished out by generations of headmasters at minor public schools. 'We're sorry you didn't win, old chap, but you were a jolly good sport.' In 2004, for example, at the Athens Olympics, it was awarded to Vanderlei de Lima, the hapless Brazilian marathon runner who was leading the race when he was attacked by a spectator and had to settle for bronze. He had not done anything particularly gallant, but the committee felt sorry for him and, because he had borne disappointment with dignity, wanted to mark its appreciation.

In Monti's case, there must also have been the sense of a

consolation prize. By 1964, he was starting to look like one of those athletes – Paula Radcliffe is another one – who dominate their event outside the Olympics, but are destined to fall short on the biggest stage. Unless his luck turned soon . . .

Mercifully, it did turn. With time running out on him, Monti only had one realistic chance of achieving his dream of Olympic gold – at the Winter Games in Grenoble in 1968, when he was already forty. But the Italian, in the form of his life, seized the moment. He took gold in both the two-man and four-man events, then retired from the sport, wreathed in glory. He was made a Commendatore of the Italian Republic, the highest civilian honour, the equivalent of a knighthood.

A sporting loser and a gracious winner. The Flying Redhead had achieved the dream double.

One man who will never forget Eugenio Monti is Robin Dixon, now Lord Glentoran, a Conservative Peer and currently shadow Olympics Minister. The gold medal he won at Innsbruck may have lost a little of its gloss – 'some of the gold has rubbed off and you can see the silver underneath' – but he acknowledges that, without the intervention of the Italian, he would not have a medal of any colour to display in his living room in Northern Ireland.

'Without the bolt he lent us, our sleigh was completely useless. He realised that, took stock of the situation and made sure that we were able to use his bolt once he had completed his own run. It was a very generous gesture, but the sort of thing people had come to expect from him.'

From the shock of red hair one imagines Monti having a flamboyant personality, but Dixon remembers him quite differently. 'Eugenio was not like that at all. You would not call him a typical outgoing Italian. He was introverted, even shy. He came from peasant stock and was not a great talker.'

In the early sixties the bobsleigh was still quite a dangerous event, and fatalities were commonplace; but that only strengthened the bonds of camaraderie between the competitors. One of Dixon's fondest memories of Monti took place in 1963, the year before the Innsbruck Olympics.

'The Italian team was having some pre-Olympic practice at Cervinia, where they had had a special bobsleigh run prepared. They had heard that Tony Nash and I were in the area, so they asked us to join them. We had to drive over the mountains through a blizzard and only got to the hotel at nine in the evening. But we could hardly have been made more welcome. The Italian mechanics got our sleigh ready in the garage, while we joined Eugenio and the others for dinner. The conversation was a mixture of Italian and pidgin English, but the wine loosened a few tongues – and the food wasn't bad either!'

For Dixon, like so many of his contemporaries, it was an age of sporting innocence. 'You don't get the same give-and-take between modern Olympians. They have to practise flat out for three or four years. They may not be technically professionals, but they have the mind-set of professionals. The pressure on them to win – simply to justify the financial investment that has been made in them – is colossal. Everything is focused on that.'

If some of the fun has gone out of sport, one thing that has never changed, as far as Dixon is concerned, is the mutual respect between top-flight athletes. 'It is very noticeable how, within a given sport, 99 per cent of the players will not have a bad word to say for each other. There is the odd exception – no names, but you can guess the sort of people I am talking about – but generally sportsmen and women the world over are united by bonds of friendship and good-will.'

The Flying Redhead may have been an exceptional sportsman, in more ways than one. But his generosity at Innsbruck mirrored a generosity that is *there*, lurking below the surface, whenever sportsmen meet to do battle.

Tana Umaga: The Two Faces of Rugby Union

Not all sporting heroes have the uncomplicated generosity of Eugenio Monti. Some zigzag between heroes and villains to the point that it is impossible to pigeon-hole them.

Sport feeds on notoriety, and, when reputations hang in the balance, it is notoriety, not sporting excellence, that wins the tie-breakers. In 2009, with our memories of Zinedine Zidane still fresh, we still prize the Frenchman for his grace and brilliance as a footballer. Come 2019, only one episode in his career will linger with any great vividness – the infamous head-butt which saw him sent off in the 2006 World Cup Final.

The Australian Greg Chappell was one of the most graceful batsmen ever to play the game. But none of his innings have endured in the way that the nadir of his career – the time when he instructed his brother to bowl the last ball of a one-day match against New Zealand underarm, to stop the opposition batsman hitting a six – has endured.

Tana Umaga, the New Zealand rugby player, is another textbook case. For a time, the Samoa-born centre was one of the most popular sportsmen his country had ever produced. But his career was destined to end on a sour note, with controversy swirling around him.

Mention the name of Tana Umaga to a rugby fan from the northern hemisphere and the episode that will surely come to mind is the infamous 'spear tackle' with which Umaga and a fellow All Black put the Lions captain Brian O'Driscoll out of the 2005 tour of New Zealand.

It was an ugly episode – quite how ugly only emerged some time later, when a video taken by a fan came to a light – and nobody came out of it with much credit, certainly not Umaga himself. If the tackle – which left O'Driscoll with a dislocated shoulder and ended his tour in the first minute of the first Test – was premeditated, Umaga and his team-mate, Kevin Mealamu, should have been red-carded. If it was just an accident, 'one of those things', why did the players not commiserate with O'Driscoll as he was being stretchered off?

Sparks flew at the time, and went on flying for weeks afterwards. The England PR machine, led by Alistair Campbell, tried to crank up the pressure on the New Zealand Rugby Football Union, who dug their heels in, refusing to accept that anything untoward had happened. One can sympathise, up to a point. Nobody likes to be browbeaten. But the NZRFU should have looked at the bigger picture. Something untoward *had* happened – 'unacceptably dangerous' was the later verdict of an International Rugby Board official on the tackle – and some graceful acknowledgement of the fact would have been welcome.

The whole episode left a nasty aftertaste. There was a feeling, in some quarters, that the All Blacks had been out of order, and had failed to accept full responsibility for their actions. When they were knocked out of the 2007 World Cup by France, despite being hot pre-tournament favourites, I was not alone in thinking that justice had been done. What goes around comes around.

But that still leaves Tana Umaga. He cannot dissociate himself from the legacy of the spear tackle, however much he might want to. 'I was perplexed by the carry-on over the Brian O'Driscoll incident,' he wrote in his autobiography, *Tana Umaga Up Close*, 'because I was thinking geez man, this is what happens in this game, so what's the fuss about? Get over it.' The words have a forlorn, disingenuous ring, as if written more in hope than expectation. Can he really not see what the fuss was about, and how close O'Driscoll came to suffering a far more serious injury? Elsewhere in the book, he calls the Irishman a 'sook', Kiwi-speak for crybaby. O'Driscoll countered with a barb of his own: 'We thought you were a gentleman.' The war of words became as unedifying as the tackle itself.

But it would be a shame if what happened in 2005 were allowed to eclipse the second most celebrated episode in Umaga's career – the moment when he showed his other, more acceptable, face.

New Zealand were playing Wales in Hamilton in June 2003 when the Welsh flanker Colin Charvis was knocked unconscious by a ferocious, though quite legitimate, tackle by Jerry Collins. These things happen when you visit New Zealand: you get off the plane, think how charming the natives are, then get trampled underfoot by rhinoceroses in rugby boots. What was one unconscious Welshmen more or less? Play swept on up the field, with the All Blacks on the attack.

Except – mercifully – for Tana Umaga, who had a ringside view of the tackle.

'It was a big, big hit, one of the biggest I had seen, and my immediate reaction was, *Yeah!* Then I saw Charvis go limp and his eyes roll back. My excitement gave way to dread. I was aware of the danger of him swallowing his mouthguard, so I just did what I had been taught: rolled him over, took out his mouth-guard and kept his tongue out of his throat. I thought I had done the right thing, but when I came off, the All Blacks doctor told me I shouldn't have moved him because he might have had a damaged neck. I asked him what I was meant to do: let him choke or take the gamble that he hadn't hurt his neck?'

If the medical professionals only gave Umaga seven out of ten, he got a perfect ten from his opponent.

'Tana was brilliant,' Charvis said later. 'I was unconscious, but he rolled me over and ensured that I didn't swallow my mouth-guard.' A potentially fatal injury had been averted.

Umaga was later presented with a commemorative figurine by the Welsh Rugby Union. He also became the first New Zealander to receive the Pierre de Coubertin Medal for good sportsmanship.

What was the score in the match? I don't remember, any more than I remember the score in the 2005 match. I imagine the All Blacks won. They usually do. Scores don't last, in the same way that an image lasts – whether it is the image of a player being stretchered off the field or the image of a player administering first aid to an opponent.

History won't forget – or entirely forgive – the O'Driscoll tackle. But, hopefully, it will also remember this other, stirring episode: a little moment of compassion in one of the toughest sports of all.

Sir Stirling Remembers

In his flat in Mayfair, a suitably pukka address for one of the gentlemen of sport, Sir Stirling Moss has surrounded himself with motor-racing memorabilia, from photographs to model cars.

In his eightieth year, the great man is as spry as ever. He is frailer than when he was in his prime, but everything about him is meticulous, from his smart-casual clothes to his immaculately organised office, not a paper out of place. His leather scrapbooks are arranged in neat chronological order, with the 'professional' ones on the top shelf and the 'personal' ones on the bottom shelf.

'The press used to take more interest in me when I was chasing girls than when I was winning races,' he jokes. It is not, however, girlfriends who peep out of one scrapbook, but a tale of quiet sporting heroism – straight-down-the-middle British honesty, 1950s style.

From the old newspaper cuttings the story of the 1958 Portuguese Grand Prix seems simple enough at first glance: 'Moss Wins in Portugal', 'Stirling Does it Again'. Just another day at the office for one of the pre-eminent racing drivers of his generation.

The only difference this time was there was a sting in the tail – a very cruel sting if you take sport over-seriously, which Moss never did.

In early reports of the race, the result is given as '1. S. Moss, 2. M. Hawthorn', Moss being followed home by his British rival Mike Hawthorn. But the plot thickens in later editions. Halfway through the race Hawthorn's car had spun off the track on to an escape road. As he tried to get it back on the main track, spectators helped him push the car – an infringement of Grand Prix rules. The Portuguese judges met to consider the incident and decided that Hawthorn would have to be disqualified or, at the very least, docked points. At which point, like a knight in shining armour, enter Stirling Moss. The great racing driver had unexpectedly acquired a new role – counsel for the defence.

'Everything was rather confused,' he remembers, 'and we were having to work through interpreters. Eyewitnesses were called to give their account of what happened. But the point I wanted to get across to the judges was that, as far as I was concerned, Hawthorn had not done anything wrong. The spectators who tried to help him did not realise they were breaking any rules: they assumed the escape lane was not part of the main track, so it was OK for them to give his car a push.'

Moss's stout defence of his rival, noted and applauded in the press, led to Hawthorn's complete exoneration. No disqualification. No points docked. But there was a heavy price to pay. At the end of the season, with savage irony, it was

Hawthorn who took the world title – by a single, tantalising point from Moss. Seldom in sporting history can such a chivalrous action have been so cruelly rewarded.

And the cruelty perpetuated itself. Throughout his career, Moss was destined – like Tim Henman in tennis, or Colin Montgomerie in golf – to play the bridesmaid, the eternal runner-up. He never did win the title, having to satisfy himself with the tag, The Best Driver Never to Win the World Championship.

Did that gall him?

'It did the first time I finished runner-up,' he admits. 'I let the disappointment gnaw away at me. But the second time it was easier, and the third time it was easier still. I realised that the most important thing was not winning, but being recognised as a good driver by my peers.'

He certainly enjoyed that recognition, becoming one of the giants of his sport: part of that select group of drivers whose names are synonymous with motor racing. While he never won the world championship, his tally of wins, in all races, was proportionally higher than that of any other driver ever. In a daredevil sport, where fatalities were commonplace, he exuded a laconic nonchalance, typified by a glorious diary entry in June 1960, after he had crashed at 140 mph: 'Shunt. Back. Legs. Nose. Bruises. Bugger.'

On the wall of his study there is a signed photograph of another legendary driver, the Argentinian Fangio, his great friend and contemporary. There was only one Fangio and there was only one Stirling Moss. At the peak of his powers – before his career was halted by a near-fatal crash in 1962 – he was one of the best-known figures in the whole country, recognised and feted wherever he went.

When policemen in the 1950s and the 1960s stopped drivers for speeding, they would ask: 'Who do you think you are? Stirling Moss?' The time when Moss himself was stopped and asked the same question has entered folklore. He lived life to the full, on and off the track, and was adored for doing it.

And if he was inclined to feel sorry for himself after what happened in Portugal in 1958, the wheel of fortune had another dramatic spin in store. Six months later, Mike Hawthorn was dead, killed in a motor accident on the Guildford bypass. The rules of Formula One had suddenly dwindled into insignificance.

'Of course, it could never happen today,' says Moss. 'I haven't changed. In the same situation, my instinct would be to do exactly the same thing. It was the right thing to do. But Formula One has changed. My team would never allow me to do something that cost the team points. There is too much money involved.'

For Moss, hero of a golden age in motor racing, the tragedy of modern Formula One is that a one-time sport – what he calls 'a gentleman's hobby' – is no longer a sport, but a commercial business. 'Don't get me wrong. I admire Lewis Hamilton hugely as a driver. But the spotlight is on him the whole time. Sponsors don't just want you to wear their logos: they want you to get involved in all sorts of events away from the track. You're selling your life to them. And the press! In my day, motor racing only made the front page when someone was killed. Otherwise it got relatively little coverage. You were not under constant scrutiny, the way you are now.'

His own generation, he insists, may have earned less money, but they had more fun. 'Our whole quality of life was better. We were so thrilled to be doing something we enjoyed and getting paid for it that we made the most of the opportunity. We had a high old time. Driving fast cars, chasing girls . . . And we competed with each other in a better spirit. I remember once travelling to Australia to take part in a big race. The axle of my car broke in practice, and I thought I was done for. But then Jack Brabham, the great Australian driver, simply said: "Take my spare axle." Problem sorted. Can you imagine that sort of thing happening today?'

If Moss regrets the decline in sporting manners, he still has the ebullience of the born winner. 'Do you see that?' he says, pointing to a model car on his mantelpiece. 'That's the Vanwall in which I won the Portuguese Grand Prix.'

The car may have shrunk. But the legend of Sir Stirling Moss, knight errant of the motor-racing world, hero to millions, one of the last survivors of a golden generation, is as large as ever.

Bobby Jones and Not Breaking into Banks

Ian Fleming knew a thing or two about sportsmanship.

The moment we realise that Goldfinger is going to be one of the creepiest of his villains is not when he tries to rob Fort Knox, or when he kills a woman by smothering her in gold paint, but when he cheats on the golf course. Unimaginable caddishness! Bond's cold fury as Goldfinger starts surreptitiously improving his lie is splendidly captured.

Golfing etiquette has its prissy aspects. It can be the most irritatingly snobbish of games. I have always despised those primmer than prim clubs where ties are mandatory in the bar and, if you change your shoes in the car park, you get a rollicking from the club secretary. But at the professional level, one can only admire the integrity with which the game is played. Cheating is not totally unknown, but, when it occurs, is like an overturning of the natural order of things.

Golfers don't cheat: they make it a point of honour not to do so, and defend that honour code with touching tenacity.

In professional tournament golf there is no great reliance on officials, still less any attempt to con or browbeat officials. Players accept responsibility for their own behaviour, sign their own score cards, own up at once if they have made a mistake. The spirit of Bobby Jones – the unofficial patron saint of golf – blows through the game like a gale.

Every sport has its dominating personalities, players who eclipse their contemporaries and set records that stand for all time. Bobby Jones belongs to an even smaller club: players who have come to define their sport and the spirit in which it should be played. The founding father of the Masters at Augusta casts almost as long a shadow over golf as W. G. Grace does over cricket. He did more than anyone to ensure that the game born on the links of Scotland became a global phenomenon, a way of life, you could almost say an attitude to life. On or off the course, he exuded decency, moral integrity. Shortly before his death – is there a tiny clue here? – he converted to Roman Catholicism.

In an era of creeping professionalism, Robert Tyre Jones Jr, born in Georgia in 1902, was the epitome of the gentleman sportsman, only playing the game for a few months in the summer. He got a B.A. in English at Harvard, then studied law. He had hinterland. One of the writers from whom he took inspiration was the Roman orator Cicero. Compared with the modern tournament professional, who goes to golf school, plays thirty-six holes a day, then retires to bed with a fat motivational tome entitled *You and Your Swing Thoughts*, he was a Renaissance Man.

He did not just play golf: he thought about golf, ruminating on its significance in the wider scheme of things. Some of his *bons mots* about the game have become legendary. 'Golf is a game of inches played between the ears.' 'No putt is short enough to be despised.' 'If you enter a tournament, and don't cheat, and happen to make the lowest score, they have to give you the cup.' 'Golf is like the game of life. You get bad breaks from good shots, you get good breaks from bad shots – but you have to play the ball where it lies.'

His reflections on sportsmanship are typically shrewd. 'I do not like an ill-natured loser. Nobody does. But I object equally to a winner or loser who makes light of the contest. Whether he has won or whether he has lost, a man owes it to his opponent to make him feel that the game has been a serious one.' Exactly. The whole context of sportsmanship, the thing that makes us treasure it when we see it, is that something important is at stake. The passion to win is what ennobles the willingness to renounce victory in a higher cause.

Jones has become such a hallowed figure that, before celebrating his genius, and in order to savour that genius the more, we should remember his feet of clay. He was a small, slightly built man and, having been a child prodigy, had the neurotic mind-set of the perfectionist. He was a chain-smoker and, during big tournaments, ate virtually nothing, losing over a stone in a week. As a young man – and he was hardly the first great golfer of whom this could be said – his temper regularly got the better of him. He once hurled his putter, nicknamed Calamity Jane, over the heads of spectators and into the bushes.

As he got older he learnt to handle the pressure, but that sense of pressure – of someone sensitive and highly strung needing to hold himself together with the whole world watching him – never deserted him. He once likened the life of a top golfer to living in a cage.

On the golf course Jones was as dominant as Tiger Woods today. In a meteoric career he won thirteen 'Majors' – the term was defined differently in those days and included the British and American Amateur Championships – before retiring at the age of twenty-eight. He would have won fourteen but for a celebrated incident at the 1925 US Open, held at the Worcester Country Club, Massachusetts.

In the first round, Jones hit his drive at the tenth hole into the rough, and was addressing his ball, surrounded by spectators, when the ball moved. Only very slightly, but it moved. At least, that is what Jones thought. Without the benefit of a TV replay, it is impossible to be sure what really happened. Certainly none of the spectators saw the ball move: if it did move, it moved so infinitesimally as to be invisible to the naked eye. The marshals also saw nothing untoward, nor did Walter Hagen, with whom Jones was playing. The unanimous opinion of those in the vicinity was that Jones had done nothing wrong and, in the interests of fairness, should receive the benefit of any doubt.

Jones – obstinately, magnificently – refused to accord himself the benefit of the doubt. He believed he had seen his ball move, so he called a one-stroke penalty on himself, in accordance with the rules.

Fate decreed that Jones, in consequence of his honesty, would lose the tournament, and by the same one-stroke margin. Without the penalty he had called on himself, Jones would have won the tournament. Instead, he tied for first place, then lost the next day in a play-off.

Fate also decreed – taking with one hand, then giving back with the other – that the name of Bobby Jones would forever be associated with nobility and self-sacrifice on the sports field. It was a tiny incident, but it swelled in significance as the years rolled by. In the minds of fans, Bobby Jones was more than a golfer: he was a gentleman.

Since 1955, the USPGA has handed out an annual award, named in his honour, for 'distinguished sportsmanship' in golf. Sportsmanship seems to have been defined with alarming laxity – recipients of the award include Bing Crosby, Bob Hope and President George Bush Sr – but it is an appropriate memorial to a man whose integrity of purpose was almost messianic.

The honesty of Bobby Jones has become so ingrained in American culture that it has even caught the attention of Hollywood. In the 2000 movie *The Legend of Bagger Vance*, directed by Robert Redford, a Jones-like character played by Matt Damon calls a penalty on himself which costs him the match. In the movie, the scene seems contrived, forced: it pales in significance compared with the real thing, a live sporting event, played in front of cheering spectators.

Certainly no Hollywood scriptwriter could have bettered the throwaway line with which Jones topped off his moment of glory.

The true sportsman not only does the decent thing but, on a point of unwavering principle, declines to take credit afterwards. That is the nature of sportsmanship: it is a state of mind, even a state of grace, from which all vanity, all self-aggrandisement, has been expunged.

Congratulated on his honesty on this occasion, Bobby Jones simply shrugged and said: 'You might as well praise a man for not breaking into banks.'

Cleveland Stroud: 'They Don't Ever Forget What You're Made Of'

If the honesty of Bobby Jones has become legendary, part of the furniture of golf, it is eclipsed, for sheer super-scrupulousness, by the honesty of Cleveland Stroud – not a household name by any means, but the embodiment of all that is most decent in small-town America.

Cleveland Stroud. The very name has a solid, dependable quality. As you roll the words around on your tongue, they seem to take you right back to the Founding Fathers, with their high ideals and unimpeachable honesty. You can trust a man called Cleveland Stroud.

Conyers, Georgia, his home town, is a community of some ten thousand souls in Rockdale County, just a short drive from Atlanta. In the nineteenth century it was a wild, unruly place: there were twelve saloons and five brothels. But modern Conyers is the acme of respectability: conservative; law-abiding; a bit sleepy. Episodes of *The Dukes of Hazzard* were filmed here. At the Atlanta Olympics, Conyers hosted the equestrian events.

To get a flavour of Cleveland Stroud – the first black man to get elected to Conyers Council – you only need to visit the council website. A smiling, bespectacled face adds substance to the cornball political promises: to keep taxes down; to keep Conyers safe; to regenerate the downtown area; to look after the sidewalks. The CV has a palpable decency.

Three children. Five grandchildren. Former 'Teacher of the Year'. Recipient of the Chamber of Commerce Life Achievement Award. Member of the Citizens' Progress Club. Twice 'Citizen of the Year' for Rockdale County. The Georgia Optimist Club 'Georgian of the Year' for 1989. You can trust Cleveland Stroud all right.

Before he was elected to the council, Stroud was basketball coach at Rockdale County High School and it was in that capacity that he briefly achieved national prominence in 1987. The Bulldogs, the team he coached, had their best-ever season, doing something they had never previously achieved, winning the Georgia boys' championship, after a dramatic coming-from-behind victory in the state finals. The whooping and hollering was over, the trophy was proudly on display at the school, in a new glass cabinet outside the gymnasium, when . . .

Oh dear. You can see catastrophe looming and, even twenty years after the event, it hurts you to watch. Those trophies in cabinets are what sport is all about. When the hurly-burly is done, when the sweat of competition is dry, they are still there; you cannot take them away. And this was a trophy which this school had never won before, had dreamed for years about winning. Every boy in the Bulldogs team must have got a buzz each time he walked past it – until Cleveland Stroud, honest Cleveland Stroud, spotted a tiny snag. No, not tiny, minuscule, no bigger than a fly on the side of that gleaming trophy.

Inter-school sports in Georgia, as in other American states, are governed by elaborate eligibility rules: you need to have passed a certain number of academic classes in order to qualify for a sports team. And it was during a routine review of grades for spring football practice that Stroud suddenly spotted that he had fielded an ineligible player in the state basketball finals. A boy who should have passed five classes the previous year had passed only four.

It was a small, inadvertent oversight, and what made it particularly galling was the fact that the boy who was ineligible had been a mere bit-part player in the team. He had come on for the last forty-five *seconds* of one match, when the Bulldogs were already leading by twenty-three points. In terms of the outcome of the match, the destination of the trophy, he was totally insignificant. If ever there was a moment to turn a blind eye . . .

But Cleveland Stroud did not, could not, turn a blind eye.

'Some people think we should have kept quiet about it,' he says, 'that it was just forty-five seconds and the player was not an impact player. But you have got to do what is honest and right and what the rules say. I told my team that people forget the scores of basketball games; they don't ever forget what you're made of.'

Stroud reported what had happened to the school principal, Henry L. Gibbs, who was horrified. 'My heart hit the floor. But there was never any question about what we had to do. We were wrong, and we had to turn ourselves in.'

The first thing Gibbs did was to write to the state basketball association. Then he went on the school's public address system to tell the students that they were probably going to lose the state title. 'I told them it was a disappointment, but we had nothing to be ashamed of. We all knew we had won those games. Then I hurried out of there. I didn't want them to see me crying.'

The trophy was returned and, although some people in Conyers were angry that the basketball association had applied the letter of the law, there was pride, locally, at the way the school had conducted itself.

'We have scandals in Washington and cheating on Wall Street,' wrote one woman in a letter to *The Rockdale Citizen.* 'Thank goodness we live in Rockdale County, where honour and integrity are alive and being practised.'

When the newspaper solicited a few hundred dollars in contributions to buy the school a replacement trophy, and medallions for the players to commemorate their winning season, the paper raised so much money it had to send some back. In disappointment, the community had pulled together. Small-town values shone brightly across a nation.

For Cleveland Stroud, who had been coach for eleven years and, before that, worked as a janitor at the school, it was a time to be philosophical, to look at the wider picture. 'They can take away the trophy, and they can take away the title, but they can't take away the fact that we won. They can't take away what we did.'

Mohammed Ali Rashwan: Wooing the Japanese

An Egyptian sportsman with cult status in Japan? Whatever next? It is hard to think of two more different countries, or of sports at which they might find themselves playing each other. Football, at a pinch, in the preliminary rounds of a World Cup. But that's about it.

But sportsmanship, even more than sport itself, transcends national boundaries. The story of Mohammed Ali Rashwan, and his love affair with the Japanese people, has a delicious simplicity: centuries of cultural differences being swept away in a matter of seconds.

Born in Alexandria in 1956, Rashwan was a top judoka, a rare beast in Egypt. As a boy, before taking up judo, he had dreamed of being a basketball star. He was a large, genial-looking man and, when not practising judo, worked as a building contractor. His career reached its climax at the 1984 Olympics in Los Angeles, where he made it through to the final in the heavyweight division, when his opponent was the great Yasuhiro Yamashita, four times world champion.

To the uninitiated, the rules of judo can be unfathomable. It is an arcane sport, and even reading about it on the web is likely to give the layman a headache. 'Yamashita's main techniques were *osoto-gari*, often executed with a hooking entry, a very strong *ouchi-gari*, which he frequently combined with a hopping *ouchimata*.' The man sounds quite terrifying, part flamingo, part charging rhinoceros.

Stockily built, and weighing in at over 280 pounds, Yamashita was revered in his own country, where he carried all before him in competition, and won his first world championship in 1979. But, after Japan boycotted the 1980 Games in Moscow, he had to wait until Los Angeles to get his first crack at Olympic gold. His legion of fans held their breath and crossed their fingers, like sports fans through the ages. They were quietly confident. The form book was on their side. But they knew that nothing in sport is certain.

Sure enough, things did not go according to plan. Yamashita tore a right calf muscle in the early rounds and, by the semi-final stage, was visibly limping. The injury put him at a huge disadvantage, as he customarily executed his throws by pivoting on his right leg. He was vulnerable to a determined, surgical opponent and fortunate that, in Mohammed Ali Rashwan, he encountered the exact opposite.

Rashwan had observed Yamashita's problems with his right leg, but decided that, in honour, he could not take advantage of them. 'It would have been against my principles,' he said afterwards. As the final got under way, he concentrated his attack on his opponent's left side, which proved a recipe for defeat. Yamashita duly won the fight and, matching chivalry with chivalry, kissed his opponent, then held his hand high in the air while the two men did a circuit of the ring together, cheered by spectators.

The story did not end there.

In the 1980s, understanding of Islam in Japan was not widespread. A Muslim judoka was an oddity in itself, but a Muslim judoka who could conduct himself with such gallantry, respecting the ancient honour codes of Japanese martial arts, immediately captured the public imagination. In downtown Tokyo, Rashwan was now the most famous

Muslim sportsman on the planet after Muhammad Ali himself, an object of fascination and admiration. His claim in an interview that his refusal to take advantage of his opponent's injury was rooted in religious principle was widely noted and applauded.

Responding to the public mood, Yamashita invited Rashwan to Japan, where he was not only welcomed like a conquering hero, but met and married a Japanese woman who converted to Islam. Others followed her example. There was a surge of interest in a culture which had previously been a closed book.

It is a lovely human story, extending far beyond the narrow confines of the judo ring. Thanks to televised sport, and a moment of unexpected generosity, a religion that had seemed alien, even threatening, received the kind of publicity which priests can only dream about.

Post 9/11, even judo has been affected by the new world order. In 2007 there was uproar in Canada when an eleven-year-old Muslim girl was not allowed to take part in a judo tournament wearing her traditional headscarf. Inter-faith suspicions have resurfaced with a vengeance. Sport, which brings people together, can also divide them.

But, from Cairo to Tokyo, the example set by Mohammed Ali Rashwan, declining to take advantage of an injured opponent, has not been entirely forgotten. It lingers in the collective memory, transcending national boundaries, reaffirming a universal truth.

In sport, as in life, you never kick a man when he is down. It is the unforgivable, unforgettable sin.

Bjornar Haakensmoen:
A Bit Syrupy?

If Japan fell in love with Mohammed Ali Rashwan, it was no more than a one-night stand compared with the passion Canada conceived for Bjornar Haakensmoen, who coached the Norwegian cross-country skiing team at the Winter Olympics in Turin in 2006.

During the six-lap sprint relay final, Haakensmoen was watching from the sidelines when the young Canadian skier Sara Renner, who was in the lead, broke her pole – the skiing equivalent of a torn Achilles. The Canadian was devastated. She had spent years training for this race. She had done all the crazy, obsessive things Olympic athletes do in pursuit of their dreams. She had even posed for a nude calendar to raise money for her team. All wasted – in a single snap.

As Renner slowed, she was passed by a Finn, a Swede, a Norwegian . . .

Haakensmoen had seen enough. He picked up one of his own poles and handed it to Renner. It was a man's pole, fifteen centimetres longer than Renner's, but the Canadian gratefully accepted the gift and started making up the lost ground. She and her relay partner Beckie Scott eventually finished second, just behind the Swedes, and took the silver medal. The Norwegian team – done out of a medal by the man who had spent years training them to win a medal – came fourth.

It is worth freezing the action there for a moment and asking: how many other sports could have accommodated such generosity? Imagine a player breaking his stick during a big ice hockey match in the States. If the opposition coach lent him a spare stick, the howls of ridicule would be heard from Oregon to Maine. The backlash from the fans would be ferocious. The coach would probably be sacked for unprofessional conduct. There is simply no room for senti- ment – or, to call it by another name, simple decency.

Haakensmoen suffered no such opprobrium. 'This is competition,' he told reporters, when questioned about his actions, 'and like all competition, it should be a fight. It should not be decided by the skis.'

Nobody in Norway, a nation known for its tolerance, had a bad word to say for him. 'They expect me to do that,' he said. 'Winning is not everything. If you win, but don't help someone when you should have, what kind of win is that? I was just helping a girl in trouble.'

If Haakensmoen was forgiven in Norway, in Canada he was a national hero. One Quebec paper published a huge 'TAKK' – Norwegian for 'thank you' – on its front page. Another suggested that every Canadian who met a Norwegian in a bar should buy them a beer. On websites, the superlatives flowed. '. . . our new Olympic hero . . . a living testament to the true meaning of sport . . . this selfless act . . . one of the brightest moments I can recall in any Olympics . . .'

One of the glories of the internet age is how intercon- nected everything has become. A small act of kindness, in a low-profile sport, can send ripples around the world. It is a cliché to say that international sport brings people together, but of all the clichés that trip off the tongues of sports fans this is the one that cannot be repeated often enough. There is no historic enmity between Canada and Norway: they are two of the most peace-loving countries on the planet. But when you see the reservoir of goodwill which a single incident can tap – nation reaching out to nation – you see the grandeur of sport.

Gifts of every description – wine, chocolate, offers of luxury hotel accommodation in Banff – winged their way across the Atlantic from Canada to Norway. As Haakensmoen achieved celebrity status, he was invited to be one of the parade marshals, alongside Sara Renner, at the annual Calgary Stampede, the world's biggest rodeo.

But the oddest gift was yet to come – five tons of maple syrup, donated by grateful Canadian fans as part of a feel-good initiative called Project Maple Syrup, organised by a Canadian businessman.

As 7400 cans of syrup rolled into Oslo – the Canadian and Norwegian governments agreed to waive import duties so that the gift would not be too expensive to accept – Haakensmoen was overwhelmed.

'When you get this kind of response, it is, well, just enormous,' he told reporters.

But did he even like maple syrup?

'It's sweet, and a little unusual,' he said, admitting that he had only just tried the syrup for the first time. 'We might have it from time to time, but not five times a day.'

Haakensmoen has since resigned as Norwegian skiing coach. But he clearly has a glittering future as a diplomat.

Paolo di Canio: The Fascist Saint

GETTY IMAGES

Some are born sporting. Some achieve sportsmanship. Some have sportsmanship have thrust upon them.

If this were a book about great sportsmen, not great sporting moments, the cast list would be entirely predictable. Bobby Charlton, Ken Rosewall, Tom Watson, Colin Cowdrey . . . Gentleman after gentleman, knights errant of the sports field, never blotting their copy book, never putting a foot wrong, never betraying the code of honour by which they played.

But part of the genius of sport is its ability to create stereotypes, then explode them. Go to a movie and you know that Johnny Depp will get the girl and the fat bastard with the scar will get killed; Hollywood is far too timid to reverse the roles. Sport, unscripted, delivers more sophisticated narratives.

When Paolo di Canio took the field for West Ham against Everton on 16 December 2000, nobody thought of him as a model sportsman, quite the reverse. The Italian midfielder had a thrilling talent, but brittle temperament. The volley against Wimbledon which won him a Goal of the Season award was one of the most brilliant ever seen in the Premier League. But he made enemies as fast as he made friends: lurching from club to club, never able to settle, always picking fights with people, from managers to team-mates.

Italian footballers can be among the most charming in the game, but Di Canio never fitted the bill. You didn't look at him and think of *gelati* and the Trevi Fountain and pretty girls on Vespas: you thought of five o'clock shadow and *mafiosi* whipping out their stilettos. There was something raw, rough-hewn about him: a coiled-spring quality. Ron Atkinson, one of his long-suffering managers, nicknamed him The Volcano.

Di Canio had grown up in a tough suburb of Rome and, as a boy, supported Lazio; he was one of the infamous *Irrudicibili*, the club's hardcore Ultra fans. Later in his career, he would be fined for making fascist salutes, and his defence ('I'm a fascist, not a racist') cut little ice. He never made any secret of his admiration for Mussolini, whose emblem he had tattooed on his arm.

His disciplinary record was wretched, and during his period in Britain – playing first for Celtic, then for Sheffield Wednesday, then for West Ham – he picked up yellow and red cards with depressing frequency. The low point came in 1998 when, after being shown a red card by Paul Alcock in a match against Arsenal, he pushed the referee to the ground, earning an eleven-game ban which many thought should have been longer. Di Canio, true to form, threw a tantrum and flew home to Italy, blaming his club for not supporting him. Thug, bad loser, spoiled brat. He was three villains wrapped into one.

Football folk shuddered at his name, the way they had shuddered when Eric Cantona launched a kung-fu kick at a fan. The assault on a match official seemed like another grim milestone on the road to anarchy. At least Cantona had been able to redeem himself on the field; for Di Canio, past thirty and playing for a mid-table club, there was not even that possibility. His place in footballing history seemed assured: an ignominious footnote.

It is worth spelling out that background to the events of 16 December 2000 in order to relish them the more. West Ham went to Everton riding high in the table. Win and they would go sixth – riches indeed for a club accustomed to relegation dogfights. But a forgettable match was fizzling out into a 1-1 draw when Di Canio got his chance. Injury time, an inviting cross from the right wing and an empty net. Any other player in the Premier League would have headed the ball home and wheeled away to celebrate the winner.

But Di Canio – his whole life at the crossroads, though he could not know it – was not any other player. Realising that the net was empty because the Everton goalkeeper, Paul Gerrard, was lying injured on the ground, having twisted his knee trying to make a clearance, he simply caught the ball and stopped play, so that the goalkeeper could receive treatment. Minutes later, the final whistle blew.

The immediate reaction was mixed. Thirty thousand Everton fans gave Di Canio a standing ovation. Harry Redknapp, his manager, was unimpressed. 'I'd be lying if I said I was happy,' he growled in a post-match interview. 'Would another club have done the same for us?' But as news of the incident spread, it was clear that, in less time than it takes to swallow a strand of spaghetti, the bad boy from Rome had gone from zero to hero. He could have scored six hat-tricks and not got such rave reviews. In an age of cynicism, his gesture in catching the ball was thrillingly unexpected.

'I'm not a saint,' the player insisted. 'During the game, the opposition is my enemy. But when they are injured, they are my colleagues and I must help them.' But sanctity, of a kind, Di Canio had surely achieved.

At the end of the year, FIFA gave the player its Fair Play Award, an obscure accolade for the very good reason that there is a dearth of credible candidates. In 1994, the award was not made at all. In 1990, pathetically, it went to Gary Lineker for not having been sent off in his career – which was a bit like giving a schoolboy a prize for not playing truant.

Di Canio, to his undying credit, not only received the Fair Play Award, but earned it, setting an example of good sportsmanship that still reverberates. He was not the first professional footballer to decline to score into an empty net because the opposition goalkeeper was injured. The Spanish player Pedro Zaballa did something similar in the 1960s. So did the French player Paul Cortin in the 1970s. But Di Canio was the first in the twenty-first century, the age when chivalry was supposed to be dead.

Football administrators, to their discredit, have tried to discourage other players from doing the same thing. They want clarity; they want consistency; they want referees to decide when to stop play because a player has been injured. But again and again, not just in the Premier League but at all levels of the game, you see footballers not waiting for the referee's whistle, but kicking the ball out of play so that an opponent can receive treatment. Common decency demands it, and footballers, whatever their other faults, do not lack common decency.

A clear honour code has evolved in recent years. If a player is injured, the ball is put out of play by the other team, then returned to the other team; then fifty thousand people clap. The code is not always strictly observed, but it is there, something quite distinct from the written rules of football. It is a kind of moral buttress in a sport that desperately needs them.

In a final delicious irony, Di Canio, the out-of-control rebel, has been proved wiser than the administrators, the guardians of fair play.

Muhammad Ali: Looking Good to God

There's not much room for gallantry in boxing: it's not that sort of sport. Respect, yes. One of the reasons the three Ali–Frazier fights are remembered as among some of the greatest encounters in all sport is the underlying professional respect the two fighters had for each other. But in the ring, with punches flying, there is no room for half measures, niceties. You just try to finish off the other guy as quickly as possible. It's not a church, it's an abattoir.

Muhammad Ali, as in so much else, bucked the trend. He could be a cruel man as well as a great boxer, often taunting opponents in a way that left a nasty taste, most notably in his 1967 fight against Ernie Terrell. But the cruelty was balanced, on occasion, by touching compassion.

When he fought Buster Mathis in Houston in 1971 the fight was such an obvious mismatch that, when the outcome was no longer in doubt, Ali deliberately went easy on his opponent, feathering Mathis with pats to the head rather than looking for the killer punch. The press didn't like the softly-softly approach, but Ali defended himself with typical eloquence.

'I don't care about all the people yelling "Kill him!"' he told reporters afterwards. 'I see the man in front of me with his eyes all glazed and his head rolling around. How do I know just how hard to hit him to knock him out and not hurt him? I don't care about looking good to fans. I want to look good to God. I got to sleep good at night. And how am I going to sleep if I kill a man in front of his wife and son just to satisfy you writers?'

The following year brought another remarkable moment of compassion, against a far more formidable opponent – Jerry Quarry.

Of the Great White Hopes who faced Ali over the years, Quarry, nicknamed the Bellflower Bomber, was one of the toughest. He cut easily, which was often his downfall, but his CV included a win against Floyd Paterson and two hard-fought encounters with Joe Frazier.

The first Ali–Quarry fight, in Atlanta in 1970, had been one of the most emotionally charged of Ali's entire career. It was his long-awaited comeback fight after being stripped of his heavyweight crown for refusing to fight in Vietnam. The fact that it was taking place in the South, simmering with racial tension, only upped the ante. Just before flying to Atlanta, Ali received a neatly wrapped box in the post. Inside was a Chihuahua which had just had its head cut off and the message 'We know how to handle black draft-dodging dogs in Georgia'. At the weigh-in, Quarry kicked up a fuss because the two doctors assigned to the fight were both black. Ali retorted that it didn't matter if Quarry had

President Nixon and the whole of the rest of the white establishment praying for him. He was still going to get whipped – and in the heart of the white South.

Feelings were running high but, below the surface, other forces – of compassion, decency, even gentleness – were also at work. A few weeks earlier, when the contract for the fight was signed, Ali had been introduced to Quarry's wife and his young son, Jerry Lynn, who clutched Ali by the hand. 'I felt disturbed in a way I can't even explain to myself,' Ali recalled later. He was a heavyweight boxer, a man of violence: he was supposed to hate, or at least give the impression of hating, his opponents. 'But how could I pretend hatred for a father whose little boy takes my hand in his, holds the fist that may smash his father's face or limit his father's fortune or ruin his reputation?'

There was a contrast, as there is with many boxers, between the outer man, all tough talk and bulging muscles, and the inner man, prey to deeper human feelings. Ali's inner man would later emerge from its cave in startling fashion.

He stopped Quarry in the third round and was hotly tipped to win the rematch in Las Vegas in 1972. Ali was privately apprehensive – he told off his backroom staff for underestimating Quarry – but turned in a typically bravura performance in the ring, picking off his opponent while, simultaneously, playing to the gallery. 'This is an easy way to earn a living,' he joked to the ringside reporters. At another point in the fight, he pretended to buckle at the knees.

By the seventh round, Quarry was out on his feet, and the fight ended in extraordinary fashion, one of those surreal sporting moments where you have to pinch yourself. Ali gently tapped his opponent with one hand and, with his other hand, frantically gestured to the referee, Mike Kaplin, to stop the fight.

Kaplin, caught off guard, stepped in and put Quarry out of his misery. Later he apologised to Ali for being slow to react. 'No heavyweight in history ever asked the referee to come save his opponent from punishment,' he explained. 'You caught me by surprise.'

A brutal sport – just how brutal time would tell, with Quarry dying of pugilistic dementia at the age of fifty-three, while Ali's fate is well known – had been illuminated by a shaft of kindness.

The aftermath of the fight, described in Ali's memoir *The Greatest*, was pretty interesting, too.

A young woman Ali had never met before came up to him in the corridor and said she was a friend of the Quarry family. Then she told him about a recurring dream she had had in the days before the fight. 'I dreamed I came up to your room and made love to you all night, every night, even the night before the fight, and when you got in the ring you were so weak he knocked you out in the third round.' After that, she burst into floods of tears.

'Greater love hath no woman than that she would lay down her virtue to guarantee a friend's victory,' Ali reflected wryly. 'Whether it would have worked for Quarry, I'll never know, but I'm glad she didn't put it to the test.'

As Ali passed Quarry's dressing room, the door was half ajar and he caught a glimpse of his opponent looking downcast. He was with his brother Mike, who had been boxing on the same bill and had also been beaten. Ali tried to go into the dressing room to console the two men, but one of Quarry's entourage saw him and closed the door in his face.

It was a sad reminder that, in the harsh world of boxing, compassion is admissible, but only in very small doses.

Nick Faldo: The Ice Man Melteth

Even in 2009 Englishmen don't hug each other. Oh, they do if they're drunk, or if they're still in their twenties, or if they've got an unexplored feminine side. But in terms of body language the hug has never been part of the national lexicon. We shake hands and leave it at that. The tactility gene has passed us by. We are a nation of Alec Guinnesses, saying it with our eyebrows.

Are we cold fish? Or are the French and the Arabs and the other hugging races warm fish? I'm not sure it really matters. The point is that, at some visceral level, we're different. If the rest of the world wants to scoff at the English for being terrified of physical contact, preferring the brisk handshake to the full-on hug, that's all right by me. All I would say – before every Englishman over thirty is marched off to the psychiatrist – is that our aversion to hugging other men has one delightful corollary. When we do hug another man, it means something. It's not a bog-standard day-to-day gesture. It has the grandeur of revelation about it.

And no hug reluctantly wrung from the withers of a cold-blooded Englishman epitomised that grandeur better than the one Nick Faldo gave Greg Norman on the last green at Augusta at the end of the 1996 Masters. I can see it still, in my mind's eye, and it still gives me a little frisson of pleasure: one of those perfect pieces of choreography that are the soul of sport.

In the history of English sang-froid Nicholas Alexander Faldo, born when Harold Macmillan was Prime Minister, deserves a chapter of his own. The man had ice in his veins. To see him chart his way around a golf course, oblivious to the crowds, oblivious to his playing partners, focused on his own game to the exclusion of all else, was an object – and chilling – lesson in single-mindedness. To his enemies, including many of his fellow professionals, he was an automaton. Couldn't he just smile occasionally? Josh with the crowds? Laugh at himself? Did winning a golf tournament have to be quite so joyless?

People wanted him to be like Ian Woosnam: one of the boys. They didn't see that, if he had been like Ian Woosnam, he wouldn't have won a single tournament. It was his emotional air-conditioning, the ability to remain cool under the severest pressure, that held the key to his success. While others faltered, he went calmly about his business.

Now that Faldo has retired from front-line competition, and we can see the man whole, it is clear that he is a far more complex, and likeable, character than people acknowledged when he was in his pomp. In the commentary box he has proved not just shrewd, but funny, capable of an irony that most golfers – a po-faced breed, it must be said – cannot match. He will never be popular with journalists. After

Europe lost the 2008 Ryder Cup under his captaincy, golf writers queued up to give him a kicking. But golf fans generally have warmed to him. They can finally see him whole – as a human being, not a machine.

But in 1996, that wryer, cuddlier Faldo lay far in the future. He was still in the business of winning golf tournaments. The ice still flowed in his veins, glacier-like, implacable.

He already had five Majors under his belt, a figure that only Seve Ballesteros, among his contemporaries, could match. But Ballesteros was a spent force. In 1996, the year before Tiger Woods burst on the scene, there was only one other golfer with a standing in the game to rival Faldo, and that was his arch-rival, Australian Greg Norman.

There had never been much love lost between the two men. That is often the way in sport. They were alpha males, predestined to fight each other tooth and claw. They came to the fore within twelve months of each other. Norman won the 1986 Open, Faldo the 1987 Open. After that, with Ballesteros on the wane, and nobody else of comparable stature on the horizon, there was a general expectation that they would go on and win more Majors. Probably Norman, the more talented of the two, would win more. So judged the experts. If only he didn't have that alarming tendency to bottle it on the final day . . .

With hindsight, the seeds of what happened at Augusta in 1996 were sown six years earlier, in the 1990 Open at St Andrews. In perfect conditions, both men played sublime golf and, at the halfway stage, were locked at twelve under par, well clear of the field. Golf fans rubbed their hands in anticipation of a classic shoot-out on the Saturday. But it never happened. Faldo, cold, remorseless, shot a 67. Norman, visibly wilting, as if demoralised by the frostiness of his playing companion, had an inglorious 76. By the end of the day, he was out of contention.

The Australian got his revenge in 1993, overhauling Faldo to take the Open at Royal St George's, but the memories of that earlier collapse clearly lingered at Augusta in 1996. Norman took a lead of six shots into the final round but, from the time he bogeyed the first hole, you could see the doubts starting to surface. What nobody could have anticipated was the extent of his disintegration. With Faldo playing faultless, though hardly scintillating, golf, Norman simply imploded. Bogeys, double bogeys, three-putts, fluffed chips, balls into the water . . . Every horror in every golfer's nightmares pursued him like an avenging Fury.

'This little old game of stick-and-ball can tear the guts out of you,' said Peter Alliss on commentary. It did not feel like a hyperbole. As the two men walked up the eighteenth fairway, with Faldo now four strokes clear, Norman looked like a ghost. He is a tall man, but, with his shoulders slumped in defeat, had the air of a whipped dog, too cowed even to whimper. The crowd stood and applauded, but with none of their usual enthusiasm; there was embarrassment written on every face. Faldo, austerely, eschewed triumphalism. He walked on to the green like an undertaker following a coffin – which, in a sense, he was.

If the golfing gods had been merciful they would have intervened at this point and let Norman birdie the final hole, to a roar of sympathetic applause. But the gods were silent, impervious. Norman did a regulation two-putt. It was Faldo, hammering the last nail in the coffin, who produced the birdie, stroking in a fifteen-footer as if it was the easiest thing in the world.

And then, suddenly, it happened. Faldo, the ice man, melted. One expected a curt handshake. That was the Faldo way. That was the only body language he knew. He was an Englishman, a child of the 1950s, a prisoner of emotional understatement, serving a life sentence. When he followed a different script, put his arms around Norman and hugged him like a long-lost brother in a spaghetti Western, it was an emotional epiphany.

The crowd, so embarrassed five minutes earlier, gave a collective sigh to relief and cheered their heads off. Faldo whispered something to Norman and the Australian, extraordinarily, gave an ear-to-ear grin. And all the pain of the day – as excruciating as anything ever witnessed on a sports field – just evaporated as if it had never been there.

Things were going to be all right. Nobody got killed. It was only a game. Someone had to lose. The sacred flame – of chivalry, of decency, of respect for a beaten opponent – burned brighter than ever.

And all because of a spontaneous, deliciously unexpected, quite un-English hug.

What did Faldo whisper to Norman as he clasped him to his chest? What did he say which produced that broad, wolfish grin? For a long time, it remained a secret: a private moment which both men wanted to remain private. The *omerta* surrounding the exchange only added to the mystique of That Hug. Then, finally, it came out. The exact words, wrote Faldo in his autobiography, were: 'I don't know what to say. Don't let the bastards get you down over this.'

There was no need to spell out who the bastards were. Faldo, more than most great sportsmen, had always had a thorny relationship with the media. After one of his Major triumphs, he famously thanked the watching press 'from the heart of his bottom'. He knew, better than anyone, that Norman would be pilloried for his last-day collapse; his nerve questioned; his frailties dissected; his whole character subjected to a sustained, pitiless onslaught. He knew that, even in the gentlemanly game of golf, nobody would think twice about kicking a man when he was down. So, like a true comrade-in-arms, he made a gesture of solidarity: just a few simple words, said half in jest, but with a wry humanity to which Norman responded.

The Australian later admitted that his opinion of Faldo had soared after the incident, which is hardly surprising. Everyone's opinion of Faldo had soared. From an awkward, sometimes graceless man had come a moment of pure sporting theatre, one of those beautifully judged gestures that count for more than the most perfect drive or the most brilliant bunker shot.

The Duchess of Kent: Grace under Pressure

To people who don't understand sport, and its rich symbolism, it probably seems the height of ludicrousness to attach significance to a golfer hugging another golfer on the eighteenth green rather than shaking him by the hand. I hope sports fans, high on the same drug as me, will better appreciate the power of a well-judged sporting gesture.

Televised sport can be every bit as asinine as other forms of televised entertainment, but it has one saving grace: the script is not written in advance. So much television, one way or another, is manipulative: pre-rehearsed, pre-packaged, to create a particular effect on the viewer. Reality show after reality show borrows from sport the competitive element – the knock-out process delivering a winner – but misses the spontaneity, the messiness, the glory of the unexpected.

I referred to the 'choreography' of Nick Faldo embracing Greg Norman. The word seemed apt, because, as it so often does, sport had suddenly achieved a balletic beauty: a drama without words, stirring the imagination. But the gesture was not choreographed, in the technical sense, and therein lay its potency. Faldo did not learn that hug on the practice range: it came from within.

When sport resorts to choreography, in nine cases out of ten it gets it pitifully wrong. Just think of the little ritual that precedes football matches in the World Cup or the Champions League: the players lining up while the anthems are played, then shaking hands before the match. As an idea, it can hardly be faulted. But in its practical application it is a nonsense. The players do shake hands with each other but, on a point of mulish professional principle, avoid eye contact. What is a handshake worth if the rest of your body is telling a different story? There is an insincerity about the ritual that jars every time.

It is the unscripted gestures – like Freddie Flintoff commiserating Brett Lee, which is where we came in – which embody the magic of sport. The crowd is sitting there expectantly, the entire focus is on the protagonists, and then, bang, one of the protagonists suddenly does something that is not just technically skilful, but morally admirable. The torch of sportsmanship has been lit.

It helps, of course, when the sporting protagonist is well known: a Flintoff, a Faldo, a Muhammad Ali. It feels as if the torch has been lit by a friend. But literally anyone can light it: a bit-part player, the referee, even someone in the crowd. All that matters, ultimately, is that someone has behaved well, in an exemplary way, in front of witnesses.

If the Faldo hug of Norman touched millions with its unexpectedness, an even more unexpected hug – overturning centuries of English protocol – lit up the stage at Wimbledon in 1998.

Normally, the person handing over the trophy at the end of a tournament is a very minor character in the drama. All the tension of the event has drained away, leaving nothing but a knees-up and a few tedious platitudes.

Once in a while the prize-dispenser fluffs his lines. Within ten minutes of the Rugby World Cup Final in 2003, when Australian Prime Minister John Howard handed over the medals to the England players like a man who had just swallowed a platypus, I was gleefully emailing my friends Down Under: 'GET RID OF THAT CONSTIPATED MISERY-GUTS! The main reason we have our own dear Queen is to *smile* on these occasions. We may have to wind her up, and change the batteries from time to time, but she has been smiling like a trouper, come rain or shine, for fifty years.'

But I doubt if even Her Majesty, after years of training, could have conducted herself better than the Duchess of Kent after the 1998 Ladies' Final at Wimbledon. It is the one we all remember, even those of us who don't watch a lot of tennis. Poor Jana Novotna, with glory beckoning, collapsing in a fit of nerves, after going two breaks up in the final set. Double fault after double fault. Wild volleys. Fluffed forehands. Backhands that barely reached the net. It was a collapse of Norman-like proportions, with Steffi Graf there to take clinical advantage, the way Faldo had. But the consolatory hug, the balm in the wound, the little gesture of kindness beamed around the world, did not come from Graf.

It was the Duchess, handing out the prizes, who was ambushed by the unexpected – Novotna sobbing uncontrollably as she received her runners-up medal – and responded perfectly, holding the tennis player as she wept.

For a brief, extraordinary moment, the two women were locked in embrace, unmoving, iconic, like figures in a medieval fresco.

Sport is full of what-ifs, and this is a textbook case. What if, let us say, the Duke of Edinburgh, or some other senior Royal from the we-don't-do-that-touchy-feely-stuff school of body language, had been handing out the prizes that day? Would they have known what to do when Novotna collapsed in tears? Or would they just have shuffled awkwardly from foot to foot, denying us, the watching millions, the gesture of consolation we craved?

The Duchess's grace under pressure was worth a thousand perfectly grooved forehands.

Sporting Sydney: The Day the Crowd Played a Blinder

EMPICS

And if a Duchess can embody sporting chivalry, why not a spectator? Why not thousands of spectators? There can be something very moving about a crowd behaving sportingly: good behaviour multiplied by a factor of X.

A lot of sports crowds are pretty unsporting, and exemplify the herd instinct at its worst, whether it is football crowds hurling abuse at the referee or tennis crowds clapping in pious approval when the umpire calls for mobile phones to be switched off.

The players themselves do not always help matters. On the eve of the 2008 Ryder Cup in Louisville, Kentucky, the American captain Paul Azinger told fans at a rally that it was OK to cheer when the Europeans missed putts. He could hardly have been more wrong. He was trampling recklessly on centuries of sporting convention. Gloating at failure turns humans into chimpanzees. There is nothing uglier than a biliously partisan crowd, baying for blood.

But there are exceptions that prove the rule. I am always touched by those one-minute silences before football matches that are perfectly observed, without a murmur of dissent. You hope it will happen, but you always fear the worst, and when your fears prove unfounded, you experience a powerful sense of relief. A well-behaved crowd of fifty thousand can restore your faith in human nature.

A home crowd applauding the opposition can also be affecting, particularly in football, where it is very rare indeed. At Old Trafford in 2003 the great Brazilian striker Ronaldo, playing for Real Madrid, could hardly believe what was happening when he was given a standing ovation by Manchester United fans, after scoring the hat-trick that dumped United out of the Champions League.

But I think, for sheer generosity of spirit, in the most testing of circumstances, the crowd at Sydney Cricket Ground on 25 February 1933 takes the prize.

In popular mythology Australian cricket crowds are among the most virulently partisan in all sport. Visiting Test cricketers have nightmares about dropping a catch on the boundary in front of the notorious Bay 20 at the MCG and getting the bird for the rest of the day. But they are neither as partisan nor as ungallant as their reputation.

The Australian batsman Matthew Hayden tells a good story about the day it was *him*, not one of the visiting players, who was copping heaps from the crowd on the boundary. 'Ey, 'ayden!' yelled a redneck in the stands at the SCG. 'Yer batting's ****!' Hayden, who had just published a celebrity cookery book, tried to ignore the man. But the barracker was not to be silenced. 'Ey, 'ayden!' he yelled. 'And, by the way, yer chicken casserole tastes like ****!'

There is an even better story in Alan Hill's biography of Herbert Sutcliffe, the great Yorkshire batsman of the inter-war period. On the 1924–5 tour of Australia, in a match in Brisbane – the most feral of Australian cities, practically a Wild West town in those days – Sutcliffe was fielding on the boundary, getting barracked by a rabble known as the Scoring Board Squad, uncomplicated Aussie souls whose idea of wit was shouting 'Yer wanted on the telephone!' when a batsman was scoring slowly. Sutcliffe, refusing to be cowed, returned their banter with interest – so much so that the Australian fans held a whip-round and, at the end of play, presented him with a case of pipes. It was inscribed: 'To H. Sutcliffe, from the Scoring Board Squad, in appreciation of his sportsmanship.'

Not that sportsmanship was high on the agenda in February 1933 . . .

One of the most infamous chapters in sporting history, the Bodyline tour, was drawing to an acrimonious close. The Australian batsmen had been battered into submission by a ferocious English pace attack spearheaded by Harold Larwood. The local hero, Don Bradman, had been cut down to size in brutal, humiliating fashion. The Ashes had been regained by an England team using tactics – fast balls directed at the batsmen, not the stumps – which dragged cricket into the gutter. No visiting team to Australia had ever been so hated – or deserved to be so hated.

If the famously partisan SCG crowd – one of the most hostile in all sport, particularly in the days of the Hill, from where raucous abuse would be directed at visiting players – had started throwing bottles on the pitch, in protest at the England tactics, nobody could have blamed them.

Instead, deliciously, they confounded the form book.

Australia batted first and were bowled out halfway

through the second day. England replied strongly, but lost a wicket just before the close of play, which necessitated the use of a night watchman. Larwood, the Australian nemesis, was told to get his pads on. The fast bowler was livid: he had been looking forward to having a shower and putting his feet up after a hard day in the field. But the England captain, the epically arrogant Douglas Jardine, was adamant. There was nothing he liked more than winding up the Australian fans, whom he regarded with undisguised disdain, and he knew that the sight of Larwood coming out to bat would send the Sydney crowd into a cacophony of booing. He was not wrong.

Larwood was so incensed at being sent in to bat that he tried to run himself out first ball. The ploy failed, and he made it through to close of play with his wicket intact. When he resumed the next morning, he was still furious and, instead of buckling down to defend, as night watchmen are supposed to, slogged merrily away, while the Australian bowlers, delighted to get some of their own back, peppered him with bouncers. Heading the queue to bowl at Larwood was H. H. 'Bull' Alexander, a hirsute, uncomplicated quickie, known to fans as the Wild Man of Borneo.

'Knock his bloody head off, Bull!' roared the fans, as he ran up to the wicket. 'Give it to the bastard!'

It must have been a riveting passage of play. The bowler batting is one of the glories of cricket. He can't bat, or not very well anyway, but he has to do his bit for his team, eking out a few runs to add to the total. And on this occasion there was a highly charged subplot. The Australian fans were not just metaphorically baying for Larwood's blood: they were literally baying for his blood. Here was the man who, throughout the series, had been bowling ferocious bouncers at the Australian batsmen and, with chilling frequency, hitting them. The bitterness engendered by the Adelaide Test, when one Australian batsman was hit on the chest and another suffered a fractured skull, was still fresh.

But the baying fans – to their great frustration – did not get the blood they wanted. Larwood slogged away, rode his luck and took the game away from Australia. After a couple of hours he was closing in on what would have been a remarkable century. Night watchmen scoring centuries are not in the script at all: it was 1962 before one of them, the Pakistani batsman Nasim-ul-Ghani, did score a century in a Test match. Larwood on this occasion fell two runs short, spooning up a catch when he was on ninety-eight.

At which point, incredibly, the fans who had been baying for his blood all morning, calling Larwood every name under the sun, rose to their feet and cheered him off the field.

Nobody was more surprised than Larwood himself. He had assumed that, as far as the Australian fans were concerned, he was the villain of the piece. He had forgotten that sports fans are creatures of conflicting emotions. Yes, they are partisan. Yes, they want their team to win. But they also, and almost as passionately, want the underdog to win. They don't cheer for Goliath: they cheer for David. And what better embodiment of David could there be than the tail-end batsman, *sans* helmet, *sans* talent, ducking head-high bouncers?

'It proved to me that Australians like a trier,' Larwood wrote in his autobiography. 'They appreciate good cricket no matter who provides it. They are tough: they barrack to unsettle a player. But they like anyone who attacks.'

No doubt class factors also crept into play. Jardine, the archetypal British toff, with his Harlequins cap, could have scored two hundred and not got a standing ovation from an

Australian crowd. In Larwood, the son of a Nottingham miner, the fans on the Hill must have recognised one of their own: a working-class scrapper who had come up the hard way.

After the war, when Larwood emigrated to Australia, and the dust of the Bodyline tour had settled, the natives embraced him like a long-lost brother. On his arrival in Sydney in 1950, he was put up in a house in the suburb of Kingsford, where he lived for the rest of his life. He did not know it, but his rent for the first few weeks was subsidised by the Australian Prime Minister, Ben Chifley. Who would have predicted that in 1933?

Larwood certainly never forgot the ovation he got after scoring ninety-eight at the SCG.

'If I had my time over again,' he wrote, 'I would score those two extra runs.'

To this day the Bodyline tour remains a low point in professional sport. For a few rancorous, hate-filled months, international goodwill was stretched close to breaking point – by an England captain who, with hindsight, put far too high a price on winning. But even the villain of the piece, Douglas Jardine, can be viewed through a kindlier lens today.

He never made it up with Don Bradman. On the 1948 tour of England, Jardine asked some of the Australian players to a drinks party. Bradman refused them permission to attend. When Jardine died in 1958, the Australian was invited to comment, but declined to do so.

Other veterans of the Bodyline series were more forgiving. 'I was thunderstruck,' wrote Bill O'Reilly, the great Australian spin-bowler, after meeting Jardine in London in 1953. 'Surely this could not be the same bloke? I liked him, and I told him so.' In middle age, Jardine became almost cuddly, laughing himself silly at *The Goon Show* and umpiring village cricket matches in a trilby, smoking a pipe.

As for good sportsmanship, the architect of Bodyline once demonstrated it in the most unlikely of settings – the press box at Lord's. Jardine was a newcomer to the press box and, not yet knowing the ropes, committed the unforgivable sin, the one a seasoned hack would blush to contemplate: he rose to his feet to clap an outgoing batsman. Applause? From a journalist? Whatever next? There was an embarrassed silence before Jardine realised his *faux pas* and resumed his seat.

The applause might have been unprofessional, but it was rooted in generosity. Scratch below the surface and one of the hardest captains in the history of sport was just one big pussy cat.

Jan Ullrich: Salvaging Something from the Wreckage

Has any sportsman had to endure quite so much frustration for quite so long as the German cyclist Jan Ullrich?

Other candidates spring to mind: Tim Henman, to name but one. There was a kind of sickening inevitability in the way, year after year, Henman would look capable of winning Wimbledon, play brilliantly in patches, get the whole nation behind him, then falter with the finishing line in sight.

Unlike Henman, Ullrich did win the big prize: the Tour de France, the Wimbledon of cycling. When he triumphed in 1997, at the age of just twenty-three, he was the first German to take the yellow jersey. Statisticians had to go back to 1947 to find a younger winner. A glittering career seemed assured. But the long years that followed, when Ullrich was beaten again and again by Lance Armstrong, but only just beaten, thus prolonging the agony, must have been a sporting Calvary.

1998, 1999, 2000, 2001 . . . The years rolled by, with the Texan simply too strong for the German, not so much physically as psychologically. Where Ullrich gave 100 per cent, Armstrong gave 110 per cent. At the highest levels of sport, it is often hunger that separates first from second. Ullrich was hungry, but Armstrong was more hungry. It was like the long-running rivalry between Chris Evert and Martina Navratilova in tennis. You watched awe-struck by the intensity of the competition. You also knew who was likely to win.

Ullrich struggled mightily to regain top spot, but the strain of being second best took its toll. He had always been criticised for being over-fond of the celebrity lifestyle, for not training properly, for putting on weight out of season. Now, little by little, he was disintegrating. In May 2002, he had his driver's licence revoked after a drink-driving incident. In June of the same year, he tested positive for amphetamine and was banned for six months, missing the 2002 Tour. A less obstinate man would have thrown in the towel.

But the obstinacy – the secret weapon of so many great sportsmen – was there. By 2003, the centenary Tour, Ullrich was back in the saddle, competing as hard as ever. The result was a classic race that would be remembered for years. Stage after stage, the battle between Ullrich and Armstrong became steadily more intense, with neither man able to gain a decisive advantage. By stage fifteen, as the riders ascended the punishing Luz Ardiden in the Pyrenees, it was still nip-and-tuck – at which point Fate, the great tie-breaker, decided to intervene, in what would become one of the most debated episodes in Tour history.

Less than ten kilometres from the end of the race, Armstrong was part of a small breakaway group that included Ullrich, when he edged too close to the spectators lining the road. His brake lever was snagged in a yellow plastic bag and he took a tumble, bringing down one of the other riders. And his problems were not over. As he remounted, his foot slipped off his pedal, he slumped over his handle bars and nearly fell for a second time.

What happened next? This being the Tour de France, probably the most consistently controversial of all major sporting events, there has never been perfect unanimity about who did what or, just as important, who should have done what.

Tour etiquette – a battered but still prized commodity, even after the years of drug scandals that had rocked the Tour – demanded that the other riders slow down to allow Armstrong to catch up. That was what had happened during the 2001 Tour, when the roles were reversed. Ullrich came hurtling off his bike during a downhill stage and Armstrong waited while he remounted. Simple courtesy called for some reciprocation.

Ullrich did reciprocate, in the sense that he slowed once he realised what had happened to Armstrong. But he did not reduce his speed very dramatically, and only slowed – depending on whose account you believe – when urged to do so by another American rider, Tyler Hamilton. Quite a few people – including Armstrong himself, in an interview after the race, when he suggested that the media had overblown 'a feel-good story' – later queried whether he had really slowed or just maintained normal race tempo. Ullrich himself has always maintained that he did slow, and that is good enough for me.

What is undisputed – and, to my mind, qualifies the German as a model of sportsmanship – is that Ullrich did not take advantage of Armstrong's fall. If ever there was a moment to attack, to take a few precious seconds out of the

American, this was it. He could – or, to the win-at-all-costs brigade, should – have surged ahead and taken the stage and, with it, the Tour itself. The margin between the two men was so slim that here, with hindsight, was the decisive moment in the race.

Instead, Ullrich held back. 'I have never in my life attacked someone who had crashed,' he said afterwards. 'That is not the way I race.' It was Armstrong, perversely, although quite legitimately, who capitalised on the situation.

The American experienced the kind of adrenaline rush that you often see in riders who have had a fall: they remount with fresh vigour, fresh determination, driving their bodies through the pain barrier. Within minutes, riding like a man possessed, Armstrong had surged ahead of Ullrich and the others, taking the stage by forty seconds, a decisive margin in the context of the race as a whole. The Tour was his, with Ullrich – again – finishing second.

For weeks debate about the episode raged among cycling fans. Had Ullrich been *too* nice? What about the incident earlier in the same Tour when Armstrong had swerved to avoid a fallen rider then taken a short cut through the corn fields? *He* hadn't stopped. Opinion became polarised and, as with all the great sporting rivalries, people divided into two camps, shrill in defence of their champion.

Neutrals like me watched slightly bemused. The Tour de France has been mired in so many scandals that it is hard to look at the event straight: you are always vaguely wondering which riders are taking which drugs; cheating and skulduggery lurk like muggers in the background. But how good that, for once, the focus had shifted away from drug-taking towards a more edifying human drama.

Ullrich, for his part, remained philosophical. 'If it happened again, I would do the same thing,' he said. 'In our

sport, which is so difficult, fair play is always written in let-
ters of gold.'

Amen to that. Some people still insist that Ullrich did not
do anything particularly praiseworthy: he just did the bare
minimum required by the unwritten rules of cycling. But I
think that is being unfair to the German.

For a winner – or, for that matter, a serial loser – to display gallantry is relatively simple. For a nearly-nearly man,
scarred by years of disappointment, to display gallantry at
the very moment when he glimpses the possibility of getting
the monkey of defeat off his back, takes true sporting grit.

Leicester City: Foxing the Bookmakers

PA PHOTOS

'It was difficult to organise because of the betting,' admitted Leicester City manager Gary Megson. 'We didn't want people to know what was going on.'

Take the quote out of context and you would assume that Megson, now manager of Bolton Wanderers, was talking about a match-fixing scandal, some grubby deal agreed in a car parked in a lay-by on the A1, with brown envelopes changing hands. Nothing so sordid. He was simply ruminating on one of the most bizarre episodes ever seen on an English football field. Sadly, it occurred in a mid-week Carling Cup replay, the kind of game only the real anoraks watch. But occur it did, and the TV cameras were there. Posterity will marvel that such daft, beautiful, surreal things could still happen in professional football in 2007.

Leicester had been drawn away to their arch-rivals

Nottingham Forest in the second round of the Cup. The stage was set for a tense East Midlands derby, with no quarter given, but the match had to be abandoned at half-time, with Forest 1-0 up, after Leicester defender Clive Clarke suffered a non-fatal heart attack. Forest could have come out for the second half but, sportingly, declined to do so. A replay was duly ordered.

To complicate matters, newly appointed Megson, who had not even been in charge of the club at the time of the initial tie, had to pick up the pieces at Leicester. His immediate priority, as he saw it, was to reciprocate the courtesy Forest had shown in agreeing to abandon the first match.

'What they did, calling the game off, was a big gesture because they were leading 1-0 and were way on top in that game. So we talked about how we should approach this new game, and we felt that it would be right and proper to make sure that the game near enough kicked off at how it had finished, at 1-0.'

Included in the discussions was club chairman Milan Mandaric, who unequivocally backed his manager. 'The idea came from the whole club – we all like to win games, but morality and fairness are also important.'

So far, so good. But there was nothing in the rules of football, no bye-law, no sound precedent, to help the Foxes achieve their objective. How, practically, does one team give another team a one-goal start? A committee of lawyers could have argued the toss all day. It was one of those unforeseen situations where administrators tie themselves in knots and it is up to the players and managers to use their common sense and cut through the red tape. A cunning plan was gradually taking shape in the Leicester dressing room, honourable in intent but shrouded in secrecy. If the bookmakers ever got wind of this one . . .

Twenty minutes before the kick-off Megson had a quiet word with his opposite number, Forest manager Colin Calderwood, and delivered what must have seemed like an early Christmas present. Leicester were going to let Forest score immediately after the kick-off, so that their 1-0 advantage from the abandoned tie could be restored. 'It was an honourable gesture,' said Calderwood afterwards. 'I was taken aback by the suggestion, but I would like to think that football came out of the game as the winner.'

Right up the last minute there was a cloak-and-dagger air to proceedings. Only after the coin toss before kick-off, Megson explained to Calderwood, would Forest be told which of their players would be allowed to score the all-important goal. He was worried that an obvious fix would leave the door open to betting irregularities. 'I didn't want there to be any suggestion of impropriety on Colin's part – or anyone at Nottingham Forest.'

After that, everything was a breeze. As soon as the game kicked off, the ball was passed to Forest goalkeeper Paul Smith – nobody had bet on *him* to score the opening goal – who was allowed to walk the ball the length of the pitch and into the Leicester net. One-nil to the Forest. As we were. Game on.

It is completely irrelevant what happened after that. For the record, Leicester City went on to win the match 3-2, securing a plum away tie to Aston Villa. They did the decent thing *and* came away with the spoils. But does anyone care about the result any more? It was only the Carling Cup. It was only one football match among thousands.

But if the score does not matter, what went on in the heads – and hearts – of Gary Megson and his players assuredly does matter. Like West Ham United, like Spurs, Leicester City has always had the reputation of a 'nice' club.

Its most famous son is Mr Nice himself, Gary Lineker. Its fans are as friendly as you could wish for. But what happened in the Carling Cup transcended niceness. It was a call to arms.

Are you watching, Liverpool? Are you watching, Chelsea? Would your club have done the same?

Shane Warne: A Gesture of Genius

I am back where I started, sitting in my favourite armchair in Oxford, looking across the room at the photograph of Freddie Flintoff consoling Brett Lee. Will I ever tire of that extraordinary image? It is nearly four years since the photograph was taken, but it has lost none of its potency, none of its capacity to raise the spirits and send a little shiver of pleasure down the spine.

Immediately above the photograph – a Christmas present from my daughter Anna – there is a framed cartoon from a 1904 *Punch*. England, captained by Pelham Warner, had just retained the Ashes in Australia. A kangaroo in cricket whites is handing over the urn to a lion in pads. Underneath there is some dialogue. British Lion: 'Think we've had most of the luck.' Australian Kangaroo: 'Not more than you deserved.'

The cartoon is more than a century older than the Flintoff–Lee photograph, but it also brings a lump to my throat when I look at it. The exaggerated courtesy – so exaggerated that the cartoonist seems to have found it mildly ridiculous – belongs to another age. But, thematically, the Edwardian cartoon and the twenty-first-century photograph belong to the same continuum: two great nations, from opposite ends of the globe, locked in chivalrous combat.

There is an empty space on the wall next to the cartoon and one day I am going to fill it with another image from the 2005 Ashes series: the last and, in some ways, grandest gesture of all.

Ninety-nine per cent of sporting scripts fall short of dramatic perfection. A thrilling football match ends with an own goal. Or a Wimbledon title is won on a double fault. There is bathos when the script demands catharsis, resolution. The extraordinary thing about the 2005 Ashes – making it, for me, a high-water mark in the history of professional sport – was that the scriptwriter never nodded. There was not a single day, or even session, which one would have wanted to unfold differently. Every piece of the narrative jigsaw fitted perfectly.

For sheer emotional intensity, the last Test was the most gripping of the five, and the last day of the last Test, with so much riding on it, was the most gripping day of the lot. By lunchtime, after a nervy morning, it looked as if the Ashes would slip from England's grasp. Three hours later, by the time Kevin Pietersen was out, victory was assured. In between, the scriptwriter had worked overtime. The post-lunch shoot-out between Lee and Pietersen – 95 mph bouncers sent soaring into the stand beneath the Oval gasometer – was the single most exciting exchange I have ever seen on a cricket field.

The scriptwriter even had time to slip in a little grace note. When Pietersen was finally out, bowled by McGrath, it was Richie Benaud's very last ball on commentary in England. What were the odds against that? It was a fairy-tale send-off for a fairy-tale innings, one of the most scintillating ever seen. This was fantasy cricket, soaring like a bird, freed from the fetters of light meters and Duckworth-Lewis and the other dreary arcana of the game.

And it was about to get even better.

As Pietersen took his leave, to the ovation of a lifetime, a figure in a white sun hat came scampering across the ground towards him. The great Shane Warne had endured a wretched day, the most wretched of his entire career. This was supposed to be his swansong, his farewell to Test cricket in England. The stage was set for him to steal the show for one last time; bowl England out; level the series; retain the Ashes for Australia. But he fluffed his lines. O, how he fluffed his lines! Not since Don Bradman got a duck in his last Test innings, on this same ground, had a great sporting chapter ended in such anti-climax.

The crucial moment came just before lunch, when Pietersen was on fifteen. An outswinger from Lee, an edge from Pietersen and a regulation slip catch for Warne. Except he didn't catch it. The ball slipped through his fingers and, as he desperately tried to grab it at the second attempt, dropped to the ground. 'Was that a moment or what?' gasped Mark Nicholas on commentary. It was a moment, Mark.

The next over, rubbing salt in the wound, the reprieved Pietersen hit Warne for two huge sixes, and he was away. The whole match, the whole series, pivoted on that single moment of fallibility.

'Warney dropped the Ashes! Warney dropped the Ashes!'

The Barmy Army, those masters of below-the-belt humour, weren't going to miss a cue like that. As Pietersen, his Hampshire team-mate, blazed his way to glory, batting with brutal brilliance, Warne had to stew in his own misery, knowing that his mistake had cost his side the match.

He was fielding on the cover boundary when Pietersen was out, and had been copping heaps from the fans behind him: good-natured, most of it, although that couldn't salve the underlying hurt. Warney had dropped the Ashes. QED.

But, like the great champion he was, he knew what he had to do.

His forty-yard jog to shake Pietersen by the hand – with the sun starting to set and the shadows of the players stretched across the Oval turf – was one of those impossibly romantic moments which sport occasionally delivers and Hollywood, with its army of emotion-milking scriptwriters, can never match. I remember watching it from my sofa in Oxford, tears pricking my eyes.

Unscripted, unrehearsed, unprompted, the gesture perfectly reciprocated Flintoff's commiseration of Lee at Edgbaston: the great Australian demonstrating that, when it came to sportsmanship, he was the equal of any Englishman. If anything, Warne had out-Flintoffed Flintoff. He had shown magnanimity, not in victory, but in the toils of a bitter, and personally bruising, defeat.

An hour later the match was over and the Ashes had been regained. For the watching England fans, scarred by years of being second best, it was a moment for unbridled celebration, full-throated yodelling. For the Australian players – none of them old enough to have played in a team that lost the Ashes – it was a time for gritted teeth and brave smiles, the kind of things that don't come easily, particularly when you are not used to doing them.

It was a test of character, not skill. Most sportsmen have the wits to know what they are expected to do when they lose, and go through the motions as best they can, trying not to sound bitter or grudging. Only a select few realise that defeat can be an opportunity as well as a disappointment. An opportunity to shine. An opportunity to make friends. An opportunity to do what professional sportsmen train to do – make something incredibly difficult seem incredibly easy through the grace of the execution.

Good sportsmanship comes in many guises. In the examples I have selected for this book one can detect certain recurring human types. There have been gracious winners, epitomised by Freddie Flintoff. There have been exemplars of honesty – Bobby Jones, Judy Guinness, Steve Kember. There have been Good Samaritans, attending to the injured – John Landy, Tana Umaga, Paolo di Canio. There have been sharers of the spoils – John Francome, Jack Nicklaus, Jean Shiley. There have been *Boy's Own* heroes – Pete Goss, Michal Krissak. There have been sportsmen who have brought smiles to our faces – Bobby Pearce, Ricky Ponting – and sportsmen who have extended the hand of friendship across national and racial divides – Lutz Long, Max Schmeling, Bjornar Haakensmoen.

But in the hierarchy of sportsmanship, top of the pile because, without him or her, sport would lose all meaning, is the good loser. Or better still, the great loser, turning losing well into an art form.

Warne in defeat was even more impressive than Warne in victory: effortlessly chivalrous; thrillingly magnanimous; supreme master of the grand, show-stopping gesture. He didn't upstage Pietersen by running to shake his hand: he played the perfect supporting role, the one the script was crying out for.

A lot of rubbish is talked and written about sport but, for me, there is no more misguided, ill-founded or obnoxious cliché in all sport than the saying, 'Show me a good loser and I will show you a loser.' The line, or variants of it, has been attributed to all sorts of people, including the famously hard-nosed American baseball coach Leo Durocher. But it has entered the lexicon of sporting psychology. It has a louche, tough-guy ring to it. And a depressing number of top sportsmen – no names, but they know who they are – seem to have adopted it as their mantra, an excuse for an uncompromising, graceless, win-at-all-costs mentality.

Not Shane Warne. He was one of the fiercest competitors who ever played the game, probably too fierce at times: he was guilty as anyone of the sledging that became a cancer in Australian cricket. But he was a great sportsman as well as a great competitor. He knew that there was a time for ferocity and a time for the opposite of ferocity – simple human kindness.

The great leg-spinner had not been able to spin his side to victory at the Oval. But like a conjuror pulling a rabbit out of a hat, he had come up with a simple, unexpected gesture in which everything that matters in sport, everything that moves us in sport, found thrilling expression.